SAINSBURY'S

HEALTHY·EATING
·COOKBOOKS·

Breads

SARAH BROWN

A committed vegetarian, yet refreshingly undoctrinaire in her approach, Sarah Brown believes in eating good healthy food and in eating well. She gives regular demonstrations and lectures, and, as national coordinator of cookery for the Vegetarian Society of the United Kingdom, runs a series of cookery courses. Well known for her highly successful BBC television series "Vegetarian Kitchen" and for her bestselling "Sarah Brown's Vegetarian Cookbook" and "Sarah Brown's Healthy Living Cookbook", she has played a major role in promoting public awareness of the link between health and diet and the widespread move towards a healthier style of eating.

SAINSBURY'S

HEALTHY·EATING
·COOKBOOKS·

Breads

SARAH BROWN

CONTENTS

INTRODUCTION 5–8

INGREDIENTS 9–20

BASIC BREADMAKING

Unkneaded bread 21, 25 • Basic wholemeal 23 • Batter method 24 • Steamed rolls 24 • Soda bread 25 • Unyeasted bread 27 • Sour dough 28

PLAIN LOAVES WITH ALTERNATIVE FLOURS

Unbleached white 30 • Malted 32, 38 • Enriched 32 • Rye 33–35 Barley 35 • Semolina 36 • Buckwheat 36 • Cracked wheat 38

SAVOURY BREAD

Herbs 39, 40, 46 • Nuts 40–43 • Rice 43 • Vegetables 40, 42, 45, 46

SWEET YEAST BAKING

Fruit and nuts 48, 50, 56 • Fruit 52 • Spiced 51–52 • Ale 54 • Honey 54

CONTINENTAL

Italian 57 • French 58–61, 65 • German 62, 66, 68 • Dutch 63

ETHNIC

Jewish 69–70, 73 • Indian 72–73 • Middle Eastern 75

QUICK BREADS, MUFFINS AND ROLLS

Quick breads 76–79 • Buns 81, 85–87 • Muffins 82–84 • Snacks 84, 88

NUTRITION CHARTS 90–93

Bread was conceived, edited and designed by Dorling Kindersley Limited, 9 Henrietta Street, London WC2E 8PS

Published exclusively for J Sainsbury plc, Stamford House, Stamford Street, London SE1 9LL by Dorling Kindersley Limited, 9 Henrietta Street, London WC2E 8PS

First published 1986

Printed in Italy

INTRODUCTION

*Delicious, inexpensive and infinitely variable, bread is fun to make,
satisfying to eat and smells marvellous. Here are a wide range of sweet and
savoury recipes – from simple rolls and traditional loaves to elaborate
Continental braids – which are suitable for lunches, parties, picnics,
teatimes and suppers.*

WHY MAKE YOUR OWN BREAD?

Wholemeal bread is one of the staples of a healthy diet as it is a valuable source of dietary fibre and unrefined carbohydrate, and is full of protein, vitamins and minerals. Home-baked breads have a marvellous flavour and also keep and freeze well. The range of shapes, tastes and textures is vast. You can make loaves, rings, cobs, plaits and individual rolls. These recipes use a whole host of ingredients; different flours, nuts, seeds, dried and fresh fruits and vegetables; and many techniques for making crusty, soft or dense loaves. You can also make salt-free and gluten-free breads. Such variety simply cannot be bought.

WHAT IS THE SECRET OF SUCCESSFUL BAKING?

Warmth is a crucial factor in successful bread-making: work in a warm kitchen if possible, have the oven pre-heated and leave dough to rise in a warm, draught-free place. The quality of the ingredients is also important. Yeast, a living organism, is the main rising agent and feeds on the flour and water in order to grow. Good quality yeast should either froth at the fermenting stage (when it is dissolved in liquid) or bubble when added to the flour. Sweeteners speed its action, but fats retard its growth, so richer doughs take longer to rise.

The main skill, however, is kneading. This is a rhythmical rocking action, designed to mix the different ingredients and make the dough smooth and elastic, activating the gluten so that the bread will rise well. It takes a while to discover your own rhythm for kneading, and it may take at least 10 minutes to get the necessary velvety texture when you are a beginner. After a little practice you will get much quicker and be able to sense when the dough has the right consistency.

Baking bread is **not** time consuming. From start to finish, it may take about 3 hours – but this is mostly long intervals in which the dough rises, proves or bakes, so there is plenty of time to do something else. Dough freezes very well, so you can make large quantities and have it readily available.

WHAT IS A HEALTHY DIET?

There now seems little question that good health is dependent on a healthy diet, no smoking and plenty of exercise. But what is a healthy diet? There seem to be a bewildering number of conflicting answers against a background of tempting new products, all advertised as "natural", "healthy" and "wholesome". What are the real facts?

FOOD FASHIONS

With the development of nutritional science over the last 100 years, the major nutrients – protein, fat, carbohydrate, vitamins and minerals – appear to have fallen in and out of favour. Shortly after the war, everyone was urged to eat more protein, but today we are told that the Western world consumes too much of this expensive energy source. Recently there has been a well-publicized debate about fats: is margarine better for you than butter? Carbohydrate, once the enemy of the slimming industry is now back in favour, as a result of the pro-fibre campaign. Yet sugar, another carbohydrate, has been blamed for tooth decay, obesity and adult-onset diabetes. Each of these fashions spawn a new "diet", which in turn encourages unbalanced eating.

GETTING THE BALANCE RIGHT

All the major nutrients have distinctive and important roles to play in our diet, and it is now clear that a healthy diet means eating not only the right quantity, but also the right type of each one (see pp.90–93).

The Western diet is very high in fat, sugar and salt, and low in fibre, fresh fruit and vegetables. The guidelines for a healthy diet, summed up by the reports prepared by the National Advisory Committee on Nutrition Education and the Committee on Medical Aspects of Food Policy are:

•Eat more unrefined carbohydrates which contain fibre (see pp.90–92).

•Eat more fresh fruit and vegetables, which contain fibre as well as vitamins and minerals.

•Eat less fat, sugar and salt (see pp. 90–92).

Adopting a healthy diet that will positively help your long- and short-term health is, therefore, only a shift of emphasis, which can quickly become a way of life.

WHAT IS WRONG WITH A HIGH-FAT DIET?

High-fat diets have been clearly linked with incidence of coronary heart disease. Moreover, a high-fat diet tends to be a low-fibre diet, which is associated with intestinal disorders, constipation, diverticulitis and cancer of the colon. One further danger – on a high-fat diet, it is easy to consume excess calories, as fat contains more than twice the number of calories, weight for weight, as carbohydrate and protein. Surplus fat is stored in the body as fatty deposits, which can lead to obesity and its attendant problems of diabetes, high blood pressure and gall bladder disease. It is important to cut down your fat intake to about 30–35 per cent of the day's calories or less. There are three types of fat, which need to be distinguished according to their origin and their interaction with cholesterol.

SATURATED FATS

Mainly found in foods from animal sources (particularly red meat fat, full-fat cheeses, butter and cream), saturated fats are high in cholesterol and if they are eaten in excess, the cholesterol can be laid down as fatty deposits in the blood vessels which can lead to heart disease and atherosclerosis.

POLYUNSATURATED FATS

These fats are mainly found in foods from vegetable sources in liquid oil form usually from plant seeds, such as sunflower and safflower. They are, however, also present in solid form in grains and nuts. Although they contribute to the overall fat intake, they can lower levels of cholesterol in the blood.

MONOUNSATURATED FATS

These fats, which are found in olive oil, have no effect on cholesterol levels, but do add to daily fat intake.

The three types of fat are present in varying proportions in high-fat foods. The fat in butter, for example, contains 63 per cent saturated fat and only 3 per cent polyunsaturated, whereas the fat in polyunsaturated margarine contains 65 per cent polyunsaturated and 12 per cent saturated fat.

WHAT IS WRONG WITH A SUGAR-RICH DIET?

Sugar, or sucrose, in the form of refined white or brown sugar is all too easy to eat, but contributes only calories to a diet. Sugar not used immediately for fuel is converted into fat, encouraging weight gain. Sugar is also a principle factor in tooth decay. Highly refined carbohydrates, particularly sugar are also absorbed easily into the bloodstream, quickly increasing blood sugar levels. If the body overreacts to this, the blood sugar levels drop dramatically, leaving the desire to eat something sweet and thus creating a vicious circle. In addition, the cells that produce insulin cannot always cope with sudden concentrations of glucose and diabetes may result. Try not only to cut down on sugar in drinks and cooking, but when cutting down, take particular care to avoid manufactured foods, both sweet and savoury, where sugar comes near the top of the list of ingredients. Always check the nutritional labelling on the container.

WHY DO WE NEED LESS SALT?

There is a clear link in certain people between salt intakes and high blood pressure – a condition that can lead to circulatory problems, such as heart disease and strokes. The sodium from salt works with potassium in regulating body fluids. Excess salt upsets this balance, which puts a strain on the kidneys. In general, we eat more salt than we need. Do be aware of the amount hidden in processed foods and try not to add more during home cooking.

WHAT IS SO GOOD ABOUT FIBRE?

High-fibre foods are more filling than other foods, take longer to chew and satisfy hunger for longer, which reduces the temptation to eat between meals. They are also less completely digested, thus helping to reduce actual calorie intake. The evidence strongly suggests that lack of dietary fibre can cause cancer of the colon in addition to simple constipation. A low-fibre diet often means a high-fat, high-sugar diet with the problems that induces, including adult-onset diabetes. Only plant foods, in the form of unrefined carbohydrates, like whole grains and fresh fruit and vegetables, contain fibre and it is critical to eat more. Simply switching to high-fibre breakfast cereals, from refined flours and pastas to wholemeal, in addition to eating plenty of fresh fruit and vegetables will dramatically increase your fibre intake.

Sarah Brown

USING WHOLEFOODS

The first step in a healthy diet is to choose fresh and wholefoods that are unrefined and as close to their natural state as possible. Simply buy plenty of fresh fruit and vegetables, and use wholemeal flour, bread, pasta and pastry and health foods and whole grains, such as beans and oatmeal. When buying convenience food, select those that contain natural ingredients and the minimum of artificial colours, flavourings and preservatives. These steps alone will ensure that your diet is high in unrefined carbohydrate, rich in vitamins and minerals and lower in fat, salt and sugar.

USING THIS BOOK

The aim of this book is to translate the simple rules for health into a practical and enjoyable form. The recipes are naturally low in fat, high in fibre and unrefined ingredients, with natural sweeteners replacing sugar. Ingredients are used in their most nutritious form.

Healthy eating is not boring, nor does it involve a sacrifice. It is simply a matter of choosing and using more nutritious foods to create delicious, yet healthy meals.

STORING FLOURS AND GRAINS

● Whole grains will keep indefinitely if stored in a cool, dry, airtight container.

● Store flours and flakes in an airtight container and use within 3–6 months before the oil in them goes rancid.

● Use wheatgerm within 2–3 weeks.

USING FRESH AND DRIED YEAST

● Fresh yeast should be smooth-textured, pleasant-smelling and beige in colour. Avoid any that is dry or crumbly with a strong smell. Fresh yeast is available in all Sainsbury stores with an in-store bakery.

● Store fresh yeast in the fridge, wrapped in polythene, and use within 10 days. It freezes well.

● Dried yeast, sold in granules, will keep for about a year. Activate by sprinkling into a cup of warm water. Stir in a little honey and leave in a warm place for 10–15 minutes.

● Leave fresh and dried yeast to ferment in a warm place.

● If using dried yeast when a recipe specifies fresh, you will need half the amount. Instant (micronised) yeast is also available.

FREEZING DOUGH AND BREAD

● Dough freezes very well. Wrap tightly in thick polythene or foil and use within 6 months.

● Freeze bread by wrapping tightly in thick polythene or foil for up to 6 weeks. Crusty bread is best used within 1 week.

● A quick way to defrost bread is to put it in a hot oven, wrapped in foil, for 30 minutes. Frozen slices of bread can be toasted straightaway. Loosen or remove wrappers when defrosting bread at room temperatures.

STORING BREAD

● Store bread loosely wrapped in polythene in a bread bin – only wrap tightly if intending to freeze. Bread stored in the fridge will go stale quickly.

● Combat mould in bread-bins by washing out regularly with a very hot solution of water and vinegar.

UNDERSTANDING THE TERMS

Fermentation: the action of the yeast on the sugar in dough.

Kneading: the rhythmic pummelling which mixes the ingredients and strengthens the gluten in the dough, enabling it to rise and prove. Knead until the dough has a velvety texture; this may take up to 10 minutes.

Rising: after kneading, the dough must be left to rise and expand.

Knocking back: after the dough has risen, it is rekneaded to ensure the yeast is evenly distributed through the dough.

Proving: a second stage at which the dough is left in a warm place to rise, before it is baked.

Gluten: a component of many flours which enables the dough to rise and prove. Salt strengthens the gluten, helping the rising action and preventing the loaf from collapsing, but as it kills yeast, must be thoroughly mixed into the flour.

Micronised yeast: an instant yeast with a long shelf life.

INGREDIENTS

Part of the joy of cooking is choosing the ingredients – especially when this involves selecting fresh fruit, herbs and vegetables and trying out new, unusual and exotic foods.

Always buy the freshest ingredients possible – they contain more vitamins and minerals and have a much better flavour and texture than preserved foods. Grains, pulses, flours, cereals and dried fruit, herbs and spices, however, generally keep for at least 3 months, so it is worth maintaining a small store of basic dry ingredients, particularly those that need to be soaked or cooked in advance. It is also useful to keep a small selection of canned or bottled fruit, vegetables and beans for emergencies. But try to select those without artificial additives or a high sugar or salt content and use them by the "best before" date.

The range of "healthy" ingredients has grown dramatically in recent years, particularly low-fat, reduced sugar, reduced salt, high fibre and vegetarian alternatives to traditional foods. These open the way to both a healthier and a more varied diet and offer endless possibilities for personal variations. The success of a recipe depends as much on the quality of the raw materials as on the way you combine them. In many cases, it is better to use a fresh alternative than to use the specified ingredient if it is not at its best – use fresh, ripe peaches, for example, in place of hard or over-ripe nectarines.

The following pages illustrate many of the familiar and the unusual ingredients found in the recipes in this book – from staples, to flavourings and dairy products. The section acts as both an identification guide and a reference source. You will find advice on choosing and storing food, together with useful information about the origins, culinary applications and nutritional value of specific ingredients. For more detailed nutritional information, see pages 90–93.

GRAINS AND FLAKES

Grains and flakes are essential staples in the diets of millions of people throughout the world. There are many alternatives to the wheat grain which we are so accustomed to in this country, and all are excellent sources of protein, minerals, oils and bran. Use grains and flakes to give a nutty, fruity texture and flavour to even the most basic loaves. Once cooked, most bread will keep for 2 days in the fridge.

OAT FLAKES

Oat flakes, normally associated with porridge, are made from whole groats which have been steamed, roasted and then rolled. Rich in minerals and B Vitamins.

MUESLI BASE

Muesli base is a combination of rye flakes, wheat flakes and oat flakes and is an excellent source of fibre and B Vitamins.

RYE FLAKES

Rye is a good source of potassium, magnesium, Vitamin B_2 and niacin. It has a distinctive, tangy flavour which is popular in bread recipes in Northern Europe and Russia.

FINE OATMEAL

Oats, once dehulled, can be rolled, flaked or ground to varying degrees of fineness. Commonly associated with oatcakes, they also make very tasty bread.

BRAN

Bran is the outer layer of a cereal and is a valuable source of fibre, protein, calcium and iron as well as a number of B Vitamins. It will enrich a wholemeal dough.

BROWN RICE

Whole grain rice is unprocessed and contains valuable nutrients. Its nutty texture and flavour combine well with a plain wholemeal dough.

COARSE OATMEAL

Oats originate from Central Europe and come flaked or ground into meal. Oatmeal is rich in protein, fibre, potassium, calcium, phosphorus and B Vitamins.

POT BARLEY

Pot barley is barley with the outer husk removed. It provides fibre, calcium, iron and phosphorus. Pearl barley is a less nutritious, more refined variety.

SEMOLINA

Semolina comes from the starchy part of wheat grain, and is available as medium or coarse meal. Most commonly used for puddings and gnocchi, it also makes a tasty loaf.

WHEAT GRAIN

Wheat grain is the most nutritious form of wheat as none of the germ or outer layers have been removed. It has a chewy, nutty texture and flavour when cooked. It is a good source of fibre, B Vitamins and minerals.

NATURAL WHEATGERM

Wheatgerm, the heart of the wheat, contains most of the major nutrients and is a rich source of protein, vitamins and minerals. Already present in unrefined wholemeal flour, it can be bought separately and will further enrich a loaf.

CRACKED WHEAT

Cracked, or kibbled, wheat is popular in the Mediterranean and Middle East. Made from the cracked berries of whole wheat, it loses bran and wheatgerm during processing. When hulled, steamed and roasted, it is known as bulgar wheat.

FLOURS

Flour can be milled from almost any cereal crop, and even from some plants, for instance potato or buckwheat. Wheat is the most popular and important bread crop in the world, due to its uniquely high gluten content. Gluten, or wheat protein, is an elastic substance which strengthens the structure of the bread, enabling it to rise during proving and baking. Gluten-free breads therefore have a much denser texture. A "strong", or high-gluten, bread has between 10 and 14 per cent wheat protein. A "soft" flour has between 7 and 10 per cent wheat protein.

BARLEY FLOUR

The gluten content of this flour is very much like that of an 85 per cent wholemeal flour, and can be used in most recipes with, or as an alternative to, wholemeal flour. It has a creamy, nutty taste.

CORNMEAL

Also known as maize flour, this high-protein flour contains no gluten, so it must be combined with a high-gluten flour such as wholemeal to make leavened bread or cakes. Yellow cornmeal, but not white, also contains Vitamin A.

RYE FLOUR

Used to make European black breads, especially pumpernickel, and to thicken sauces and vegetable soups. It contains magnesium, iron and B-group Vitamins.

POTATO FLOUR

A low-gluten flour usually used with wholemeal flour for baking, or alone as a thickening agent. A good source of unrefined starch and Vitamins A, B_2, B_6, E and folic acid.

GRANARY-TYPE FLOUR

A specially formulated wheatmeal flour which has a small quantity of malted wholemeal to improve moistness and keeping quality. Excellent toasted.

BUCKWHEAT FLOUR

Buckwheat is not a cereal, but a plant
related to rhubarb and sorrel, which can be
ground to a meal and used in baking. Its
seeds are also available and can be roasted
before use. Buckwheat is rich in protein.

WHOLEMEAL FLOUR

A high-gluten flour, extensively used in all
kinds of baking, and recently to make pasta. It
can be combined with other flours for variety
and is a good source of fibre, E and B Vitamins.
The Vitamin E goes rancid eventually, so use
within 2–3 months.

SOYA FLOUR

Use this alone or with wholemeal flour for
thickening or baking – if thickening it can
replace eggs, since it is very high in protein.
High in polyunsaturated fats, mineral salts and
E and B Vitamins.

CHAPATTI FLOUR

Made from half plain and half wholemeal flour,
it makes round Indian breads, which are flat
because no yeast activates the gluten.

STRONG WHITE/UNBLEACHED WHITE FLOUR

A "strong" flour is a high-gluten flour containing
10–14 per cent wheat protein, or gluten.
White flour is made from the endosperm (what
is left when the husk and germ are removed). It
contains iron, calcium, niacin and Vitamin B_1.

FRUIT AND NUTS

*Fruit and nuts are valuable sources of nutrients, providing a wide range
of vitamins and minerals. Both help to increase fibre intake, and nuts
also add protein and polyunsaturated fats. Unshelled nuts will keep for
up to 6 months and shelled ones for up to 3 months. Dried fruit, stored
in an airtight tin, keeps for about a year. A piece of citrus fruit in the tin
will keep it moist.*

BLACK OLIVES

There are several varieties of olive
and they can be bought fresh and
pickled, whole, pitted and stuffed.
Black olives are fully ripened, unlike
the green ones.

SULTANAS, RAISINS, CURRANTS

Raisins and sultanas are dried
white grapes and currants are
dried black ones. They are a rich
source of Vitamin B_6 and
potassium, and their natural
sweetness is very useful in
healthy baking.

DRIED FIGS

Figs, an excellent source of fibre, are
available fresh in summer and autumn, and
dried all year. Dried figs are rich in niacin
and Vitamin B_6, calcium, iron, sodium,
potassium and magnesium.

FRESH DATES

The succulent flavour and texture of fresh dates
makes them a useful addition to a bread dough,
giving it moisture and sweetness. They are
available all year round.

COOKING APPLES

The tart flavour of Bramley apples
(above) complements both sweet and
savoury loaves.

CASHEW NUTS

Cashew nuts have a soft,
creamy texture and delicate
flavour, and are a good
source of B Vitamins
and calcium.

HAZELNUTS

Hazelnuts are readily available unshelled,
shelled, chopped and ground. They are a good
source of Vitamins B_1, B_6 and E.

GROUND ALMONDS

Ground, flaked and chopped, almonds
complement sweet and savoury loaves.

WALNUTS

Walnuts, widely available,
make an excellent ingredient in
a loaf and a tasty garnish.

ORANGE

Rich in Vitamin C
and folic acid, and
invaluable for their
texture, colour,
flavour, rind and juice.

BANANAS

Fibre-rich bananas are a tropical fruit,
containing folic acid and Vitamin B_6.
They contribute moisture and natural
sweetness to bread doughs.

LIQUIDS, FLAVOURINGS ~AND~ SWEETENERS

Natural flavourings can take the form of spices, sweeteners and even alcohol. Added to a bread or cake dough, they can boost the vitamin and mineral content, while simultaneously enriching the flavour and colour of the finished loaf.

NUTMEG

Nutmeg, native to Indonesia, can be bought whole and ground.

CINNAMON STICKS

Sweet-tasting cinnamon, the dried bark of an Indian tree, is available as sticks or powder.

CAROB POWDER

Carob powder is a low-calorie, low-fat, caffeine-free alternative to cocoa. It is also sweeter than cocoa and is ideal in baking.

ALLSPICE

Allspice, the dried berry of the Jamaican pepper tree, tastes like a combination of cloves, cinnamon and nutmeg.

CONCENTRATED APPLE JUICE

Apple juice, a low-calorie, natural sweetener, is slightly piquant and therefore works well in sweet and savoury baking.

BROWN SUGAR

Brown sugar is not unrefined as is often thought, but does contain some added minerals and has a distinctive, treacly flavour.

STOUT ALE

Stout ale is a heavy-bodied ale, made from roasted and flaked barley, hops, malt and water.

MUSCOVADO SUGAR

This is a partly refined sugar with a strong, distinctive flavour.

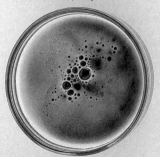

CIDER

Cider is made from fermented apple juice and makes a delicious, fruity-tasting loaf.

CLOVES

Cloves are buds of an evergreen tree and have a strong, distinctive flavour which combines well with citrus fruit.

MOLASSES

Molasses, a cane sugar product, contains calcium, iron and some B Vitamins. Its strong flavour combines well with ginger and fruit in baking.

HONEY

There are many types of honey available, all of them remarkably different in texture. The flavour varies according to the source of the pollen.

MAPLE SYRUP

This rich sweetener is made from sugar maple and black maple and is very concentrated. It contains calcium and is less sweet than honey.

MALT EXTRACT

Malt extract, also called barley syrup, is less sweet than sugar and is an excellent natural sweetener to use in baking.

OLIVE OIL

Olive oil is a good source of mono-unsaturated fat and Vitamin E, and has a rich flavour and colour. "Virgin oil" is the best quality olive oil available.

VANILLA ESSENCE

This is the highly concentrated extract of the vanilla pod and its characteristic flavour is ideal in sweet baking.

RUM

Rum is distilled from sugar cane and molasses and produced mainly in the West Indies. It works well in sweet doughs.

DAIRY PRODUCTS, ALTERNATIVES ~ AND RAISING AGENTS

Dairy products enrich the texture and flavour of a loaf and are an important element in the more elaborate recipes, suitable for teatime and special occasions They also increase the protein, vitamin and mineral content of a loaf. However, they do not need to be high in fat, as you can make use of low-fat alternatives, such as skimmed milk, buttermilk, low-fat soft cheese (quark, for example).

BUTTERMILK

Buttermilk is made from pasteurized skimmed milk and a culture. Low in fat, it is a useful alternative to sour cream and milk.

YOGURT

Yogurt is made from curdled milk and originates from Turkey. Its mild, tangy taste and smooth texture make it a useful ingredient in breadmaking, and it is also a rich source of protein and calcium.

EGGS

Brown and white hens' eggs have the same nutritional value. The egg yolks contain cholesterol and lecithin, a substance which helps to carry fats round the body. The egg whites contain protein only.

SKIMMED MILK SOFT CHEESE
(quark)

Quark is a low-fat, protein-rich, soft cheese made from skimmed milk. It has a mild flavour and creamy texture which makes it a versatile ingredient in any recipe. Use as a healthier alternative to cream cheese.

SKIMMED MILK

Skimmed milk has only 1 per cent of the fat and half the calories of whole milk, but is just as rich in B_2, B_{12}, calcium and protein.

DRIED YEAST

Dried yeast is the most convenient form of yeast. Re-activate by soaking in warm water and a little sugar for 10–15 minutes.

MICRONISED YEAST

A type of dried, instant yeast that does not need reconstituting and is quicker to act than ordinary dried yeast. Many of the commercial brands have added ascorbic acid (Vitamin C) to speed up the reaction time further.

BICARBONATE OF SODA

When combined with an acid such as buttermilk or yogurt, bicarbonate of soda (or sodium bicarbonate) becomes a raising agent.

FRESH YEAST

Buy fresh yeast in small quantities as it soon loses its potency. When fresh, it should be pale beige with a smooth surface and a pleasant smell.

CHEDDAR CHEESE

Reduced-fat and rennet-free versions of this traditional English cheese are also available. An excellent source of protein, Vitamins A, B_2, B_{12}, D and folic acid, calcium and zinc.

BAKING POWDER

Baking powder is a combination of cream of tartar, bicarbonate of soda and salt, and is used as a raising agent in breadmaking.

SEEDS

*Seeds are an excellent source of protein and polyunsaturated fat.
They give a crunchy texture and rich flavour to savoury
breads, sweet loaves and rolls, and make a good garnish.*

LINSEEDS

Linseeds come from the flax plant and
were eaten by the Greeks and Romans.
Believed to have soothing properties,
they are popular in savoury baking.

POPPY SEEDS

Poppy seeds are available white and
blackish-blue. Native to the
Middle East, they are particularly
popular in Indian and
Jewish baking.

ANISEEDS

Aniseeds originated in Greece and
Egypt, and can be used in powdered
as well as seed form. They have
a distinctive, liquorice flavour
which is popular in Mexican and
Mediterranean cooking.

CORIANDER SEEDS

Coriander seeds have a mild yet
spicy flavour and are widely used in
curries. They are best bought whole
and can then be left whole, or
crushed just before using.

SUNFLOWER SEEDS

Sunflower seeds are very
rich in proteins and
minerals. They supply E
and B Vitamins,
particularly Vitamin B_1,
and are rich in iron. They
combine well with other
seeds and nuts in baking.

CARAWAY SEEDS

Caraway seeds originated in Asia and
their distinctive flavour is very popular,
particularly in German, Austrian and
Jewish baking.

CUMIN

Cumin is important in Middle Eastern,
Indian and Moroccan cuisine. Its warm, spicy
scent and rich flavour combine well with bread.

SESAME SEEDS

Sesame seeds contain iron, A and
B Vitamins, and are particularly
rich in calcium. Excellent in ethnic
and sweet loaves, and as a garnish.

CELERY SEEDS

Celery seeds have a slightly bitter
taste that goes well with the texture
and flavour of a wide range of
breads, particularly something
sharp and tangy like pumpernickel
(see p. 62).

BASIC BREAD MAKING

Breadmaking need not be a complicated business, once you have mastered the basic techniques. Using unrefined flour makes a loaf rich in carbohydrate, protein and fibre as well as valuable vitamins and minerals. Many of these loaves are quick to prepare and can be left to rise and prove while you do other things.

BREAD
WITH NO KNEADING

INGREDIENTS

1½ lb (750g) wholemeal flour
1 packet instant yeast
1 tsp (5ml) salt
1 tsp (5ml) brown sugar
2–2¼ pints (1.2–1.4l)
warm water

•

NUTRITION PROFILE

This bread is rich in protein, magnesium, iron, zinc, fibre, niacin and Vitamins B$_1$ and B$_6$.

• Per loaf •
Carbohydrate: 166g
Protein: 34g   Fibre: 25g
Fat: 5g   Calories: 805g

Since the dough is not kneaded and the yeast is instant (or micronised), this bread is extremely quick to make. Some brands of this new type of yeast contain Vitamin C (ascorbic acid) which helps the rising process. Breads which are quick to make do not have the same flavour as more slowly fermented doughs and do not last as long.

Preparation time: 45 mins   Cooking time: 40 mins
Makes approx three 1 lb (500g) loaves

METHOD

1. Mix the flour with the yeast, salt and sugar in a bowl.

2. Add 2 pints (1.2 litres) of the water. Mix together very thoroughly, then add a little more water if necessary so that the dough holds together. It should be on the wet side.

3. Divide the dough into three well-greased 1 lb (500g) loaf tins and leave to rise.

4. Once the dough has risen to the size of a finished loaf, it is ready to bake.

5. Bake in a preheated oven at Gas Mark 6, 400°F, 200°C for 30 minutes, then remove from the tin and bake for a further 10 minutes. Cool on a wire rack.

Illustrated on page 22

BASIC WHOLEMEAL BREAD

INGREDIENTS

1oz (25g) fresh yeast
1 tsp (5ml) molasses
1oz (25g) soya flour
¾ pint (450ml) warm water
1½ lb (750g) wholemeal flour
1 tsp (5ml) salt
1 tbsp (15ml) sunflower oil

•

NUTRITION PROFILE

This loaf is an excellent source of protein, niacin, Vitamins B$_1$ and B$_6$, magnesium, zinc, iron and fibre.

• Per loaf •
Carbohydrate: 235g
Protein: 52g   **Fibre:** 35g
Fat: 18g   **Calories:** 1240

This standard recipe is the basis for many variations. The addition of oil and soya flour improves the texture, but increases the fat.

Preparation time: 1½ hours   Cooking time: 35–40 mins
Makes two 1 lb (500g) loaves or one 2¼ lb (1kg) loaf approx

METHOD

1. Stir the yeast, molasses and soya flour together until creamy. Pour on ¼ pint (150ml) of the warm water and whisk vigorously until the yeast dissolves. Leave in a warm place for 5–10 minutes to ferment. A froth will form on the surface.

2. Mix the flour with the salt in a warm dry bowl. Pour the yeast mixture over the flour. Add the remaining water and oil. Stir with a wooden spoon until the dough starts to form (see below). Knead well for up to 10 minutes until the dough becomes smooth.

3. Transfer to a clean bowl, cover and leave the dough to rise in a warm place for about 1 hour until it has doubled (see below).

4. Take the dough out of the bowl and knock it back. Knead again for a few minutes. Divide the dough in half and shape into loaves. Place in two greased 1 lb (500g) loaf tins, or shape the dough into one large loaf and place in a greased 2 lb (1kg) loaf tin. Leave to prove for 15–20 minutes.

5. Bake in a preheated oven at Gas Mark 7, 425°F, 220°C for 35–40 minutes (20 mins for rolls). The bread is done if it sounds hollow when tapped on the base. Cool on a wire rack.

Illustrated on page 26

BASIC WHOLEMEAL BREAD

It takes less time to make bread than you might think, because most of the preparation time is in fact the rising and proving time. The delicious smell and nutty texture of freshly baked, homemade, wholemeal bread make it well worth the effort. You can always shape the dough into rolls instead of a loaf for variety.

1. Mix the flour and salt. Pour on the yeast mixture. Add the remaining water and oil and stir into a dough.

2. Knead the dough for 10 mins. Transfer to a clean bowl. Cover with clingfilm and leave to rise for 1 hour.

3. Knock back the dough and knead briefly. Mould the dough into a loaf or rolls.

From top: **Batter method wholemeal bread** (*see p. 24*); **Bread with no kneading** (*see p. 21*); **Steamed sesame rolls** (*see p. 24*).

BATTER METHOD WHOLEMEAL BREAD

INGREDIENTS

1oz (25g) fresh yeast
¾ pint (450ml) warm water
1½ lb (750g) wholemeal flour
1 tsp (5ml) salt
1 tbsp (15ml) sunflower oil

•

NUTRITION PROFILE

This loaf is a good source of fibre, niacin, Vitamins B₁ and B₆, iron, magnesium, zinc and protein.

• Per loaf •
Carbohydrate: 494g
Protein: 102g   Fibre: 74g
Fat: 30g   Calories: 2535

This technique is useful when using a mixture of high-gluten and low-gluten flours (such as rye or buckwheat), and for unsweetened breads.

Preparation time: 1½ hours   Cooking time: 25–35 mins
Makes one 2¼ lb (1kg) loaf or two 1 lb (500g) loaves approx

METHOD

1. Whisk the yeast and water. Leave in a warm place for 5–10 minutes to ferment. Stir in half the flour and mix to a batter. Cover with clingfilm or a cloth and leave for 30 minutes. Add the remaining flour, salt and oil. Work to a dough and knead.

2. Shape the dough into one or two loaves. Place in a greased 2 lb (1kg) loaf tin or two 1 lb (500g) tins. Cover and leave to prove for 20–30 minutes. Bake in a preheated oven at Gas Mark 7, 425°F, 220°C for 25–35 minutes. Cool on a wire rack.

Illustrated on page 22

STEAMED SESAME ROLLS

INGREDIENTS

½oz (15g) fresh yeast
1 tbsp (15ml) clear honey
8 fl oz (250ml) warm water
12oz (375g) wholemeal flour
1 tbsp (15ml) sesame seeds
2 tsp (10ml) sesame or olive oil

•

NUTRITION PROFILE

These high-fibre rolls are rich in niacin, Vitamins B₁, B₆ and E, iron, magnesium, zinc and protein.

• Per roll •
Carbohydrate: 41g
Protein: 8g   Fibre: 6g
Fat: 4g   Calories: 220

Steaming produces bread with a very light, spongy texture and a soft crust – ideal for rolls. It also enhances the flavour of the wheat, which suits a salt-free recipe such as this. The rolls are best eaten within a day.

Preparation time: 1 hour   Cooking time: 25 mins
Makes approx 6–7 rolls

METHOD

1. Whisk the yeast, honey and half the water together. Leave in a warm place for 5–10 minutes to ferment.

2. Mix the flour with the sesame seeds in a bowl. Pour over the yeast mixture, oil and remaining water. Work to a smooth dough. Knead well. Transfer to a clean bowl. Cover with clingfilm or a cloth and leave to rise for 15 minutes.

3. Knock back and knead briefly. Divide into 3oz (75g) pieces, shape into rolls, cover and leave to prove for 10–15 minutes.

4. Transfer on to wet muslin or a tea towel. Cover and steam in a steamer or pan for 15 minutes. Turn off the heat and leave for 10 minutes. Cool on a wire rack.

Illustrated on page 22

SODA BREAD

INGREDIENTS

1 lb (500g) wholemeal flour
1 tsp (5ml) bicarbonate of soda
2 tsp (10ml) salt
½ pint (300ml) buttermilk
•

NUTRITION PROFILE

*Soda bread contains fibre, niacin,
Vitamins B₁ and B₆, calcium, iron,
magnesium, zinc and protein.*

• Per loaf •
Carbohydrate: 349g
Protein: 79g **Fibre:** 47g
Fat: 10g **Calories:** 1715

*A basic soda recipe is very quick to make and is best eaten warm. It is
important to bake the bread immediately the dough is mixed, as the
bicarbonate of soda starts to act as soon as it is wet.*

Preparation time: 15 mins   Cooking time: 45–50 mins
Makes one large 1½ lb (750g) cob or two small ¾ lb (375g) cobs approx

METHOD

1. Sift the flour with the soda and salt into a bowl. Pour in the
buttermilk and mix to a soft dough. Add a little warm water
if necessary.

2. Shape into one large cob or two small ones. Mark a cross in the
top of each. Place on a greased and floured baking sheet.

3. Bake in a preheated oven at Gas Mark 7, 425°F, 220°C for 30
minutes, then reduce the oven temperature to Gas Mark 6,
400°F, 200°C and bake for a further 15–20 minutes. Cool.

Illustrated on page 26

GRANT LOAF

INGREDIENTS

½oz (15g) fresh yeast
13 fl oz (375ml) warm water
1 tsp (5ml) brown sugar
1 lb (500g) wholemeal flour
1 tsp (5ml) salt
•

NUTRITION PROFILE

*This loaf is a good source of fibre, niacin,
Vitamins B₁ and B₆, iron, magnesium,
zinc and protein.*

• Per loaf •
Carbohydrate: 335g
Protein: 67g **Fibre:** 48g
Fat: 10g **Calories:** 1615

*This loaf derives its name from Doris Grant, the author of a well-
known bread book, who developed the recipe. The dough is made very
wet and is scarcely kneaded. The resulting loaf has a dense crumb and
thick crust. This is an excellent recipe for anyone baking in a hurry.*

Preparation time: 45 mins   Cooking time: 35 mins
Makes approx one 1½ lb (750g) loaf

METHOD

1. Dissolve the yeast in 3 tbsp (45ml) of the water. Leave for 2
minutes, then stir in the sugar. Leave in a warm place for a few
minutes to ferment.

2. Mix the flour with the salt in a bowl. Pour over the yeast
mixture and remaining water. Mix with a wooden spoon.

3. Beat very well – the consistency should be wet and sticky.
Spoon into a greased 2 lb (1kg) loaf tin. Cover with clingfilm or a
cloth and leave to rise for 20 minutes.

4. Bake in a preheated oven at Gas Mark 7, 425°F, 220°C for 35
minutes. Cool on a wire rack.

Illustrated on page 26

UNYEASTED BREAD

INGREDIENTS

8oz (250g) wholemeal flour
½ tsp salt
6oz (175g) cooked barley or rice
8–10 fl oz (250–300ml) hot water

•

NUTRITION PROFILE

*This loaf is a good source of fibre, niacin,
Vitamin B₁, zinc and protein.*

• Per loaf •
Carbohydrate: 200g
Protein: 34g **Fibre:** 23g
Fat: 5g **Calories:** 930

*It is essential to leave this dough to rise for a long time so that the
natural yeasts have time to develop. This moist bread keeps well.*

Preparation time: 1¼ hours (plus 24 hours' rising time)
Cooking time: 30–40 mins
Makes approx one 1¼ lb (625g) loaf

METHOD

1. Mix the flour with the salt in a bowl. Stir in the cooked barley or
rice. Pour over the hot water and mix in. Knead carefully, leaving
the dough quite sticky. Transfer to a clean bowl. Cover with
clingfilm or a cloth and leave in a warm place for 24 hours to rise.

2. Knead again briefly. Shape into a loaf. Place in a greased 1 lb
(500g) loaf tin. Cover and leave to prove for 45–60 minutes.

3. Bake in a preheated oven at Gas Mark 7, 425°F, 220°C for
30–40 minutes. Cool on a wire rack.

Illustrated opposite

VITAMIN C LOAF

INGREDIENTS

1oz (25g) fresh yeast
1 tsp (5ml) molasses
1oz (25g) soya flour
¾ pint (450ml) warm water
25mg Vitamin C tablet
1½ lb (750g) wholemeal flour
1 tsp (5ml) salt
1 tbsp (15ml) sunflower oil

•

NUTRITION PROFILE

*This loaf is an excellent source of Vitamins
B₁, B₆ and C, niacin, protein,
magnesium, zinc, iron and fibre.*

• Per loaf •
Carbohydrate: 235g
Protein: 52g **Fibre:** 35g
Fat: 18g **Calories:** 1240

*A Vitamin C tablet speeds up the action of the yeast and reduces rising
and proving times, making this a very quick and pleasantly sweet loaf.*

Preparation time: 1 hour   Cooking time: 35–40 mins
Makes approx two 1 lb (500g) loaves

METHOD

1. Stir the yeast, molasses and soya flour together until creamy.
Pour on ¼ pint (150ml) of the warm water and whisk vigorously.
Crush the Vitamin C tablet and mix it into the yeast mixture.
Leave in a warm place for 5–10 minutes to ferment.

2. Mix the flour and salt in a warm dry bowl. Pour the yeast mixture
over the flour. Add the remaining water and the oil and stir with a
wooden spoon until the dough starts to form. Knead well.

3. Transfer to a clean bowl. Cover with clingfilm or a cloth.
Leave to rise until it has doubled. Knock back and knead again.

4. Divide and shape the dough into two. Place in two greased 1 lb
(500g) tins and leave to prove. Bake in a preheated oven at Gas
Mark 7, 425°F, 220°C for 35–40 minutes. Cool on a wire rack.

Illustrated on page 29

Clockwise from top left: **Soda bread** (*see p. 25*); **Grant loaf** (*see p. 25*); **Basic wholemeal bread** (*see p. 23*);
Unyeasted bread (*see above*); **Basic wholemeal rolls** (*see p. 23*).

BASIC SOUR DOUGH RYE BREAD

INGREDIENTS

SOUR DOUGH STARTER
4oz (125g) rye flour
4 fl oz (125ml) skimmed milk
$\frac{1}{2}$ tsp salt

DOUGH
2oz (50g) fresh yeast
16 fl oz (475ml) warm water
1 lb (500g) rye flour
2 tsp (10ml) caraway seeds
2 tsp (10ml) salt
8–10oz (250–300g) wholemeal flour

•
NUTRITION PROFILE

*This bread is a good source of Vitamins B$_1$
and B$_6$, iron, magnesium, protein, fibre
and zinc.*

• Per loaf •
Carbohydrate: 325g
Protein: 48g   **Fibre:** 44g
Fat: 12g   **Calories:** 1515

Keep this bread for at least one day before eating.

Preparation time: 1 hour (plus 3 days for the dough to sour)
Cooking time: 1$\frac{1}{4}$–1$\frac{1}{2}$ hours
Makes approx two 1 lb (500g) loaves

METHOD

1. For the sour dough starter, mix the rye flour, milk and salt
together. Cover and leave in a warm place for 48 hours to sour.

2. For the dough, dissolve the yeast in $\frac{1}{2}$ pint (300ml) of the
warm water and mix in the sour dough. Add half the rye flour and
caraway seeds, stir in well. Cover and leave overnight.

3. Mix the remaining rye flour and salt. Add to the dough with
the remaining warm water and the wholemeal flour. Knead well.

4. Form the dough into two cob shapes. Place on greased and
floured baking sheets. Cover with clingfilm or a cloth and leave to
rise for 45 minutes. Bake in a preheated oven at Gas Mark 6,
400°F, 200°C for 1$\frac{1}{4}$–1$\frac{1}{2}$ hours. Cool on a wire rack.

Illustrated opposite

SOUR DOUGH RYE BREAD
WITH COTTAGE CHEESE

INGREDIENTS

SOUR DOUGH STARTER
2oz (50g) rye flour
4oz (125g) cottage cheese
2 tbsp (30ml) warm water

DOUGH
1oz (25g) fresh yeast
4oz (125g) rye flour
1$\frac{1}{2}$ tsp (7.5ml) salt
8oz (250g) wholemeal flour

•
NUTRITION PROFILE

*This loaf is rich in Vitamins B$_1$ and B$_6$,
iron, magnesium, protein, fibre and zinc.*

• Per loaf •
Carbohydrate: 299g
Protein: 67g   **Fibre:** 43g
Fat: 14g   **Calories:** 1515

This loaf has a light texture and mild tangy flavour.

Preparation time: 1$\frac{1}{2}$ hours (plus 24 hours' standing time)
Cooking time: 40–45 mins
Makes approx one 1 lb (500g) loaf

METHOD

1. For the sour dough, mix the rye flour, cottage cheese and warm
water. Leave to stand in a fairly warm place for 24 hours to sour.

2. For the dough, dissolve the yeast in $\frac{1}{4}$ pint (150ml) of warm
water. Mix with the sour dough. Leave in a warm place for 15
minutes. Mix the flours and salt, add to the sour dough. Knead.

3. Shape the dough into a sausage loaf shape. Place on a greased
baking sheet. Prick well, cover and leave for 45 minutes. Bake in
a preheated oven at Gas Mark 6, 400°F, 200°C for 40–45
minutes. Cool on a wire rack.

Illustrated opposite

Clockwise from top left: **Basic sour dough rye bread** (*see above*); **Sour dough rye bread with cottage cheese** (*see above*);
Vitamin C loaf (*see p.27*).

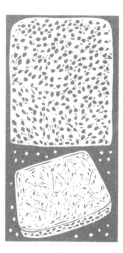

PLAIN LOAVES
WITH
ALTERNATIVE FLOURS

There is no need to stick to wholemeal flour when breadmaking. Take advantage of the wide range of cereals now available, such as cracked wheat, barley, oatmeal and buckwheat, to come up with delicious, unusual combinations.

UNBLEACHED WHITE PLAITED RING

INGREDIENTS

1oz (25g) fresh yeast
1 tbsp (15ml) clear honey
¾ pint (450ml) warm water
1½ lb (750g) unbleached white flour
1 tsp (5ml) salt
1 tbsp (15ml) sunflower oil

GLAZE (optional)
a little beaten egg

•

NUTRITION PROFILE

This loaf is rich in Vitamin B₁, calcium, protein and iron.

• Per loaf •
Carbohydrate: 577g
Protein: 91g   **Fibre:** 24g
Fat: 26g   **Calories:** 2775

After using wholemeal flour, white dough feels pliable, easy to handle and rises well. It can taste bland, so if you want white bread to complement a light soup or summer salad, choose a good quality unbleached white flour, and add a little oil to improve the dough.

Preparation time: 1½ hours   Cooking time: 25–30 mins
Makes approx one 2½ lb (1.2kg) loaf

METHOD

1. Whisk the yeast, honey and ¼ pint (150ml) warm water together. Leave in a warm place for 5–10 minutes to ferment.

2. Mix the flour with the salt in a bowl. Pour over the yeast mixture, the remaining warm water and sunflower oil and knead well, adding more flour or liquid if necessary. Transfer to a clean bowl. Cover with clingfilm or a cloth and leave to rise for 30–40 minutes.

3. Knock back and knead again briefly. Divide the dough into three pieces. Roll each piece into a very long rope. Plait the pieces together, then fold the ends of the plait in towards the centre to make a 'B' shape. Place on a greased baking sheet. Cover and leave to prove for 20–25 minutes. Brush with egg.

4. Bake in a preheated oven at Gas Mark 7, 425°F, 220°C for 25–30 minutes. Cool on a wire rack.

Illustrated opposite

Clockwise from top left: **Enriched wholemeal with poppy seeds** (*see p.32*); **Unbleached white plaited ring** (*see above*); **Granary cob** (*see p.32*).

GRANARY COB

INGREDIENTS

½oz (15g) fresh yeast
2 tbsp (30ml) malt extract
8–10 fl oz (250–300ml) warm water
8oz (250g) wholemeal flour
8oz (250g) granary-type flour
1 tsp (5ml) salt
1 tbsp (15ml) sunflower oil

GARNISH
1–2 tbsp (15–30ml) kibbled or
cracked wheat

•

NUTRITION PROFILE

*This bread is rich in niacin, Vitamin B₁,
iron, zinc and magnesium.*

• Per loaf •
Carbohydrate: 387g
Protein: 69g **Fibre:** 47g
Fat: 26g **Calories:** 1965

*Granary-type flour is a wheatmeal flour containing some malted whole
wheat grains. Granary bread is a healthy, versatile loaf.*

Preparation time: 1½ hours   Cooking time: 25–35 mins
Makes approx one 1½ lb (750g) cob

METHOD

1. Whisk the yeast, malt extract and about half the water
together. Leave in a warm place for 5–10 minutes to ferment.

2. Mix the flours and salt in a bowl. Add the yeast mixture, the
remaining water and the oil. Knead well. Transfer to a clean
bowl. Cover with clingfilm or a cloth and leave to rise for 20–30
minutes. Knead, shape into a cob, then dip in cracked wheat.
Place on a greased baking sheet. Cover and leave for 20 minutes.

3. Bake in a preheated oven at Gas Mark 7, 425°F, 220°C for
25–35 minutes. Cool on a wire rack.

Illustrated on page 31

ENRICHED WHOLEMEAL WITH POPPY SEEDS

INGREDIENTS

¾oz (20g) fresh yeast
1 tbsp (15ml) clear honey
½ pint (300ml) warm water
1 lb (500g) wholemeal flour
1 tsp (5ml) salt
2 tbsp (30ml) soya flour
2 tbsp (30ml) skimmed milk powder
2 tbsp (30ml) wheatgerm
2 tbsp (30ml) ground almonds
2 tbsp (30ml) oat flakes

GARNISH
a little beaten egg
1–2 tbsp (15–30ml) poppy seeds

•

NUTRITION PROFILE

*This bread is rich in fibre, niacin, Vitamins
B₁, B₆ and E, calcium, iron, magnesium,
zinc and protein.*

• Per loaf •
Carbohydrate: 195g
Protein: 51g **Fibre:** 30g
Fat: 17g **Calories:** 1085

*There are many ways to enrich a basic dough – skimmed milk powder,
nuts, seeds, as well as flakes and flours. This recipe produces a nutty-
tasting loaf with a dry crumb.*

Preparation time: 1½ hours   Cooking time: 25–35 mins
Makes approx two 1 lb (500g) loaves

METHOD

1. Whisk the yeast, honey and warm water together. Leave in a
warm place for 5–10 minutes to ferment.

2. Mix the flour with the salt, soya flour, milk powder,
wheatgerm, ground almonds and oat flakes. Stir in the yeast
mixture. Knead well, adding more flour or liquid if necessary.
Transfer to a clean bowl. Cover with clingfilm or a cloth and
leave to rise for 35–40 minutes.

3. Knead again lightly. Divide the dough in half and shape into
loaves. Place in two lightly greased 1 lb (500g) loaf tins. Cover
and leave to prove for 20 minutes. Brush with beaten egg and
sprinkle with poppy seeds. Bake in a preheated oven at Gas Mark
7, 425°F, 220°C for 25–35 minutes. Cool on wire racks.

Illustrated on page 31

BATTER-METHOD RYE BREAD
WITH SMETANA

INGREDIENTS

½oz (15g) fresh yeast
1 tbsp (15ml) molasses
7 fl oz (200ml) warm water
8oz (250g) wholemeal flour
8–10oz (250–300g) rye flour
1 tsp (5ml) salt
3 fl oz (75ml) smetana or soured cream
2 tbsp (30ml) sunflower oil
1 tbsp (15ml) caraway seeds

•

NUTRITION PROFILE

*This bread is a good source of fibre,
Vitamins B₁, B₆ and E, iron, magnesium,
zinc and protein.*

• Per loaf •
Carbohydrate: 376g
Protein: 61g   **Fibre:** 34g
Fat: 49g   **Calories:** 2095

*This bread is made using the batter method as this gives the yeast a
chance to work with the high-gluten wholemeal flour before being mixed
with the low-gluten rye flour.*

Preparation time: 2 hours   Cooking time: 25–35 mins
Makes approx one 1¾ lb (875g) loaf

METHOD

1. Whisk the yeast, molasses and water together in a large bowl.
Leave in a warm place for 5–10 minutes to ferment.

2. Stir in half the wholemeal flour, and mix to a thick batter.
Cover and leave the yeast to activate for 30 minutes.

3. Mix the remaining ingredients with the batter yeast mixture
(see below). Work to a smooth dough and knead well, adding
more flour or liquid if necessary.

4. Transfer to a clean bowl. Cover and leave to rise for
30–40 minutes.

5. Knock back and knead again briefly. Shape the dough into a
long sausage shape. Place on a greased baking sheet. Cover with
clingfilm or a cloth and leave to prove for 20 minutes. Prick well.

6. Bake in a preheated oven at Gas Mark 7, 425°F, 220°C for
25–35 minutes. Cool on a wire rack.

Illustrated on page 34

MAKING BATTER-METHOD RYE BREAD WITH SMETANA

*Breads made with low-gluten flours such as rye do not always rise well. Making a batter of wholemeal flour
and water in which the yeast can ferment before being kneaded with the low-gluten flour solves this problem
and speeds up the fermentation process.*

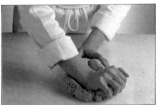

1. Stir half the wholemeal flour into the
fermented yeast mixture. Mix to a thick
batter. Cover and leave to rise.

2. Mix together the rest of the
wholemeal flour, rye flour and salt. Add
to the yeasted batter mixture.

3. Add the smetana, oil and caraway
seeds. Work to a smooth dough, knead
well and leave to rise for 30–40 mins.

RYE <small>AND</small> OATMEAL COB

INGREDIENTS

$\frac{1}{2}$oz (15g) fresh yeast
1 tbsp (15ml) clear honey
2 tbsp (30ml) soya flour
$\frac{1}{2}$ pint (300ml) skimmed milk and
warm water
8oz (250g) wholemeal flour
4oz (125g) rye flour
4oz (125g) coarse oatmeal
1 tsp (5ml) salt
2 tsp (10ml) mixed spice
1 tbsp (15ml) sunflower oil

•

NUTRITION PROFILE

*This cob loaf is rich in fibre, Vitamins B_1
and B_6, iron, magnesium, zinc and
protein.*

• Per loaf •
Carbohydrate: 376g
Protein: 78g **Fibre:** 40g
Fat: 38g **Calories:** 2065

The combination of grains in this cob adds extra flavour and nutrients.

Preparation time: $1\frac{3}{4}$ hours Cooking time: 25–35 minutes
Makes approx one $1\frac{3}{4}$ lb (875g) cob

METHOD

1. Whisk the yeast, honey, soya flour and $\frac{1}{4}$ pint (150ml) of the warm milk and water. Leave for 5–10 minutes to ferment.

2. Mix the wholemeal flour, rye flour, oatmeal, salt and mixed spice in a bowl. Add the yeast mixture with the remaining liquid and the oil. Knead well adding more flour or liquid if necessary. Transfer to a clean bowl. Cover with clingfilm or a cloth and leave to rise for 30–40 minutes.

3. Knead again briefly. Shape the dough into a large cob. Clip the top with a pair of scissors to make a cross. Place on a greased baking sheet. Cover and leave to prove for 20 minutes. Bake in a preheated oven at Gas Mark 7, 425°F, 220°C for 25–35 minutes. Cool on a wire rack.

Illustrated opposite

BARLEY <small>AND</small> LINSEED LOAF

INGREDIENTS

$\frac{1}{2}$oz (15g) fresh yeast
1 tbsp (15ml) clear honey
8–10 fl oz (250–300ml) warm water
1 tbsp (15ml) sesame oil
4oz (125g) barley flour
8oz (250g) wholemeal flour
$\frac{1}{2}$ tsp salt
3 tbsp (45ml) linseeds
1 tbsp (15ml) sunflower oil

GARNISH
1–2 tbsp (15–30ml) linseeds

•

NUTRITION PROFILE

*This loaf is a good source of protein, fibre,
niacin, Vitamins B_6 and E, magnesium
and zinc.*

• Per loaf •
Carbohydrate: 272g
Protein: 61g **Fibre:** 35g
Fat: 65g **Calories:** 1885

Barley flour produces a marvellous loaf with a light nutty flavour.

Preparation time: $1\frac{3}{4}$ hours Cooking time: 25–35 mins
Makes approx one $1\frac{1}{4}$ lb (625g) loaf

METHOD

1. Whisk the yeast, honey and about half the water together. Leave in a warm place for 5–10 minutes to ferment.

2. Heat the sesame oil in a pan and gently toast the barley flour. Mix the barley flour, wholemeal flour, salt and linseeds in a bowl. Pour over the yeast mixture, remaining water and oil. Knead, then transfer to a clean bowl. Cover and leave to rise for 30 minutes.

3. Knead again briefly. Shape the dough into a long sausage shape. Roll in extra linseeds. Place on a greased baking sheet. Cover and leave to prove for 20 minutes. Prick well. Bake in a preheated oven at Gas Mark 7, 425°F, 220°C for 25–35 minutes. Cool on a wire rack.

Illustrated opposite

From top: **Batter-method rye bread with smetana** (*see p. 33*); **Barley and linseed loaf** (*see above*);
Rye and oatmeal cob (*see above*).

SEMOLINA PLAIT WITH CUMIN

INGREDIENTS

2 tbsp (30ml) cumin seeds
1/2oz (15g) fresh yeast
2 tbsp (30ml) soya flour
3fl oz (75ml) warm water
12oz (375g) wholemeal flour
4oz (125g) semolina
1 tsp (5ml) salt
2 tbsp (30ml) olive oil
6 tbsp (90ml) natural yogurt

GLAZE
a little beaten egg

•

NUTRITION PROFILE

This plait loaf is a good source of fibre, niacin, Vitamins B_1 and B_6, iron, magnesium, zinc and protein.

• Per loaf •
Carbohydrate: 348g
Protein: 81g   Fibre: 37g
Fat: 55g   Calories: 2115

Olive oil, soya flour and yogurt give the dough a velvet texture.

Preparation time: 1¾ hours   Cooking time: 25–35 mins
Makes approx one 1½ lb (750g) plait

METHOD

1. Lightly roast the cumin seeds in a heavy frying pan for a few minutes. Leave to cool. Whisk the yeast, soya flour and warm water. Leave in a warm place for 5–10 minutes to ferment.

2. Mix the flour, semolina and salt in a bowl. Pour over the yeast mixture, oil, yogurt and 2 tsp (10ml) of the cumin seeds. Knead well. Transfer to a clean bowl. Cover and leave for 35–40 minutes.

3. Knead again briefly. Divide the dough into 3. Roll into 12–15 inch (30–37cm) lengths. Plait and put on a greased baking sheet. Cover and leave for 20–25 minutes. Glaze with beaten egg and the remaining cumin seeds. Bake in a preheated oven at Gas Mark 7, 425°F, 220°C for 25–35 minutes. Cool on a wire rack.

Illustrated opposite

BUCKWHEAT LOAF WITH GINGER

INGREDIENTS

1/2oz (15g) fresh yeast
2 tsp (10ml) brown sugar
1 tbsp (15ml) soya flour
8–10 fl oz (250–300ml) warm water
12oz (375g) wholemeal flour
4oz (125g) buckwheat flour
1 tsp (5ml) ground ginger
1 tsp (5ml) salt
2 tsp (10ml) grated orange rind
2 tbsp (30ml) olive oil
a little beaten egg
2 tbsp (30ml) sesame seeds

•

NUTRITION PROFILE

This loaf is a good source of Vitamins B_1 and B_6, iron, magnesium, zinc, niacin.

• Per loaf •
Carbohydrate: 329g
Protein: 75g   Fibre: 52g
Fat: 55g   Calories: 2065

Buckwheat flour produces loaves with a dark colour and quite a dry texture, which is countered by adding some oil to the dough.

Preparation time: 1¾ hours   Cooking time: 25–30 mins
Makes approx one 1½ lb (750g) loaf

METHOD

1. Whisk the yeast, sugar, soya flour and half the water together. Leave in a warm place for 5–10 minutes to ferment.

2. Mix the flours with the ginger, salt and orange rind. Add the yeast, the remaining water and the oil. Knead well, adding more flour or liquid if necessary. Transfer to a clean bowl. Cover with clingfilm or a cloth and leave to rise for 20–30 minutes.

3. Knead briefly. Shape into a loaf. Place in a greased 2 lb (1kg) loaf tin. Cover and leave to prove for 20 minutes. Glaze with beaten egg and sesame seeds. Bake in a preheated oven at Gas Mark 7, 425°F, 220°C for 25–30 minutes. Cool on a wire rack.

Illustrated opposite

From top: **Kibbled wheat bread** (*see p.38*); **Semolina plait with cumin** (*see above*); **Malted oatmeal cob** (*see p.38*); **Buckwheat loaf with ginger** (*see above*).

KIBBLED WHEAT BREAD

INGREDIENTS

4oz (125g) kibbled or cracked wheat
8 fl oz (250ml) boiling water
1 tbsp (15ml) molasses
½oz (15g) fresh yeast
4 fl oz (125ml) warm water
14oz (425g) wholemeal flour
1 tsp (5ml) salt

GARNISH
extra kibbled or cracked wheat

•

NUTRITION PROFILE

This high-fibre loaf is a good source of niacin, Vitamins B₁ and B₆, iron, magnesium, zinc and protein.

• Per loaf •
Carbohydrate: 374g
Protein: 74g **Fibre:** 54g
Fat: 11g **Calories:** 1800

Kibbled or cracked wheat is the uncooked grain lightly crushed by a mechanical process. It gives the bread extra texture and moisture.

Preparation time: 2 hours   Cooking time: 25–35 mins
Makes approx one 1¼lb (625g) loaf

METHOD

1. Pour the boiling water over the kibbled wheat and stir in the molasses. Leave to cool. Whisk the yeast and warm water together. Leave in a warm place for 5–10 minutes to ferment.

2. Mix the flour with the salt in a bowl. Pour over the yeast mixture and add the kibbled wheat plus the soaking liquid. Mix, then knead well. Transfer to a clean bowl, cover with clingfilm or a cloth and leave for 30–40 minutes.

3. Knead again briefly. Shape the dough into a loaf. Sprinkle with kibbled wheat. Place in a greased 1 lb (500g) loaf tin. Cover and leave for 20 minutes. Bake in a preheated oven at Gas Mark 7, 425°F, 220°C for 25–35 minutes. Cool on a wire rack.

Illustrated on page 37

MALTED OATMEAL COB

INGREDIENTS

½oz (15g) fresh yeast
1 tbsp (15ml) malt extract
¼ pint (150ml) warm water
12oz (375g) wholemeal flour
4oz (125g) medium oatmeal
½ tsp salt
½ tsp grated nutmeg
3–5 fl oz (75–150ml) warm milk

•

NUTRITION PROFILE

This cob loaf is a good source of fibre, niacin, Vitamins B₁ and B₆, iron, magnesium, zinc and protein.

• Per loaf •
Carbohydrate: 346g
Protein: 68g **Fibre:** 43g
Fat: 19g **Calories:** 1740

The malt and nutmeg are more dominant when this bread is toasted.

Preparation time: 1½ hours   Cooking time: 30–35 mins
Makes approx one 1½lb (750g) cob

METHOD

1. Whisk the yeast, malt extract and water together. Leave in a warm place for 5–10 minutes to ferment.

2. Mix the flour with the oatmeal, salt and nutmeg. Pour over the yeast mixture with 3 fl oz (75ml) of the warm milk. Work to a smooth dough and knead, adding more milk if necessary. Transfer to a clean bowl. Cover and leave for 35–40 minutes.

3. Knead again briefly. Shape the dough into a large cob. Place on a greased baking sheet, cover and leave to prove for 20–25 minutes. Bake in a preheated oven at Gas Mark 7, 425°F, 220°C for 30–35 minutes. Cool on a wire rack.

Illustrated on page 37

SAVOURY BREAD

Bread can be much more than a bland staple to pad out a
meal or soak up some leftover sauce. The loaves in this
section show that, imaginatively combined with nuts,
seeds, herbs, spices, and vegetables, savoury loaves can play
an exciting and tasty part in a meal, and can be
very nutritious.

HERB BREAD
IN A FLOWER POT

*For special occasions or just for a change, try baking bread in a clean,
dry, earthenware flower pot to make a pyramid-shaped loaf. This high-
fibre, herb recipe can be adapted to include any herbs you like.*

Preparation time: 2 hours   Cooking time: 40–45 mins
Makes approx one 1½ lb (750g) loaf

INGREDIENTS

½oz (15g) fresh yeast
½ pint (300ml) warm water
1 lb (500g) wholemeal flour
½ tsp salt
2 tbsp (30ml) soya flour
4 tbsp (60ml) fresh mixed herbs,
finely chopped

GLAZE
a little beaten egg
1–2 tsp (5–10ml) sesame seeds

•

NUTRITION PROFILE

*This loaf is a good source of iron,
magnesium, zinc, protein, fibre, niacin
and Vitamins B_1 and B_6.*

• Per loaf •
Carbohydrate: 334g
Protein: 81g   **Fibre:** 54g
Fat: 21g   **Calories:** 1765

METHOD

1. Whisk the yeast and warm water together and leave in a warm
place for 5–10 minutes to ferment.

2. Mix the wholemeal flour with the salt and soya flour in a large
bowl. Add the herbs and mix well.

3. Pour on the yeast mixture and work to a dough. Knead well.
Transfer to a clean bowl, cover with clingfilm or a cloth and leave
to rise for 30–45 minutes.

4. Knock back and knead again briefly. Shape into a round and
place in a well greased flower pot. Leave to prove for about
30–45 minutes.

5. Brush with beaten egg and sprinkle with sesame seeds. Bake in
a preheated oven at Gas Mark 7, 425°F, 220°C for 40–45
minutes. Turn out on to a wire rack. Serve hot or cold.

Illustrated on page 41

SUNFLOWER AND WALNUT LOAF

INGREDIENTS

¹/₂oz (15g) fresh yeast
8–10 fl oz (250–300ml) warm water
12oz (375g) wholemeal flour
1 tsp (5ml) salt
2oz (50g) sunflower seeds, ground
2oz (50g) walnut pieces, chopped
4oz (125g) oat flakes
2 tbsp (30ml) wheatgerm

GARNISH
oat flakes

•

NUTRITION PROFILE

This bread is high in fibre and protein, and a good source of zinc, magnesium, iron, Vitamins B₁, B₆ and E, and niacin.

• Per loaf •
Carbohydrate: 336g
Protein: 82g **Fibre:** 49g
Fat: 69g **Calories:** 2200

Walnuts add a savoury flavour to this nourishing high-fibre bread, and together with the sunflower seeds, boost the protein, vitamin and mineral content. A good bread to serve with salads or soups.

Preparation time: 1¹/₂ hours   Cooking time: 30–35 mins
Makes approx one 1³/₄ lb (875g) loaf

METHOD

1. Whisk the yeast and warm water together. Leave in a warm place for 5–10 minutes to ferment.

2. Mix the flour with the salt, ground sunflower seeds, walnuts, oat flakes and wheatgerm in a bowl. Pour over the yeast mixture. Work to a smooth dough and knead well, adding more flour or liquid if necessary. Transfer to a clean bowl, cover with clingfilm or a cloth and leave to rise for 35–40 minutes.

3. Knock back and knead again briefly. Shape the dough into a large sausage shape. Roll in oat flakes. Place on a greased baking sheet. Cover and leave to prove for 20–25 minutes. Bake in a preheated oven at Gas Mark 7, 425°F, 220°C for 30–35 minutes. Cool on a wire rack.

Illustrated opposite

DAKTYLA WITH OLIVES AND PARSLEY

INGREDIENTS

1 lb (500g) basic dough (see p.23)
2oz (50g) stoned black olives
3 cloves garlic, crushed
¹/₂oz (15g) fresh parsley,
finely chopped

GLAZE
a little beaten egg
2–3 tbsp (30–45ml) sesame seeds

•

NUTRITION PROFILE

This loaf is a good source of protein, fibre, niacin, Vitamins B₁ and B₆, iron, magnesium and zinc.

• Per loaf •
Carbohydrate: 232g
Protein: 56g **Fibre:** 37g
Fat: 31g **Calories:** 1365

This is a bloomer-shaped loaf, scored crossways into fingers (or "daktyla" in Greek) and sprinkled with sesame seeds.

Preparation time: 30 mins (plus 1¹/₂ hours for making the basic dough)
Cooking time: 25–30 mins
Makes approx one 1 lb (500g) loaf

METHOD

1. Roll out the dough into a short thick oblong. Using your fingertips, make several indentations. Scatter over the chopped olives, garlic and parsley. Roll up into the dough. Knead briefly. Shape into a long sausage and make several deep, diagonal cuts across the loaf. Place on a greased baking sheet.

2. Cover and leave for 20 minutes. Brush with beaten egg and sprinkle thickly with sesame seeds. Bake in a preheated oven at Gas Mark 7, 425°F, 220°C for 25–30 minutes. Cool on a wire rack.

Illustrated opposite

Clockwise from top left: **Herb bread in a flower pot** (*see p.39*); **Daktyla with olives and parsley** (*see above*); **Sunflower and walnut loaf** (*see above*).

CASHEW ~ CARROT BRAID

INGREDIENTS

½oz (15g) fresh yeast
⅓ pint (200ml) warm water
14oz (425g) granary-type flour
1 tsp (5ml) salt
1–2 tsp (5–10ml) dried marjoram
1 tbsp (15ml) olive oil

FILLING

1 tbsp (15ml) olive oil
1 medium onion, peeled and
finely chopped
8oz (250g) carrots, peeled and very
finely diced
3oz (75g) unsalted cashew nut pieces
2 tbsp (30ml) shoyu
2 tbsp (30ml) apple chutney
freshly ground black pepper

GLAZE

a little beaten egg
1 tbsp (15ml) crushed coriander seeds

•

NUTRITION PROFILE

*This high-fibre loaf is a good source of
Vitamins A, B₁ and C, niacin, folic acid,
magnesium, iron and protein.*

• Per loaf •
Carbohydrate: 330g
Protein: 71g **Fibre:** 53g
Fat: 80g **Calories:** 2260

*Bread dough makes an unusual and healthy alternative to pastry for
savoury as well as sweet fillings. Nutritious granary-type flour is used
here; it contains malted grains of wheat and rye. Use this versatile
recipe with its moist cashew and carrot filling for a picnic spread, a
lunch buffet, or as a supper dish with soup.*

Preparation time: 1¾ hours   Cooking time: 25–35 mins
Makes approx one 1¾ lb (875g) loaf

METHOD

1. Whisk the yeast and ¼ pint (150ml) of the warm water
together. Leave in a warm place for 5 minutes to ferment.

2. Mix the flour with the salt and marjoram in a bowl. Pour over
the yeast mixture, olive oil and the remaining warm water. Work
to a smooth dough and knead well (see opposite), adding more
flour or water if necessary.

3. Transfer to a clean bowl. Oil the surface of the dough, cover
with clingfilm or a cloth and leave to rise for 20 minutes.

4. For the filling, heat the oil in a pan and gently fry the onion for
10–15 minutes until soft but not coloured. Add the carrots and
cashew nuts, cover and cook for 5 minutes, stirring occasionally.

5. Remove from the heat and stir in the shoyu and chutney.
Season to taste with black pepper.

6. Knock back the dough and knead briefly. Roll out to an
oblong. Place the filling down the centre. Make diagonal slits in
the dough, either side of the filling, about 1 inch (2.5cm) apart.
Weave the slices over the filling (see opposite).

7. Place the braid on a greased baking sheet. Cover and leave to
prove for 20 minutes. Brush with beaten egg and sprinkle with
crushed coriander seeds.

8. Bake in a preheated oven at Gas Mark 7, 425°F, 220°C for
25–35 minutes. Serve warm or cold.

Illustrated on page 44

MAKING A BRAID

Braided, or plaited loaves are often made with an enriched dough, but brown bread makes an unusual and healthier alternative. A loaf which is visually interesting and attractive can take a more prominent place on a dinner or buffet table. The filling can be adapted to complement the other dishes.

1. Combine the flour, seasoning, fermented yeast mixture, oil and water. Work to a smooth dough and knead well.

2. Place the filling down the centre of the rolled-out dough, making diagonal slits on either side.

3. Weave the slices of dough over the filling. Glaze with beaten egg and coriander seeds before baking.

RICE BREAD

INGREDIENTS

$^1/_2$oz (15g) fresh yeast
8 fl oz (250ml) warm water
12oz (375g) wholemeal flour
$^1/_2$ tsp salt
2 tsp (10ml) brewer's yeast
1 tbsp (15ml) shoyu
1 tbsp (15ml) sunflower oil
8oz (250g) cooked brown rice

•

NUTRITION PROFILE

This loaf is a good source of fibre, niacin, Vitamin B_1, zinc and protein.

• Per loaf •
Carbohydrate: 300g
Protein: 57g **Fibre:** 40g
Fat: 25g **Calories:** 1585

Cooked grains, especially rice, add moisture and texture to a plain wholemeal dough. They make the loaf stay fresh for longer, and contribute extra fibre. This loaf is dense and heavy, so cut thin slices.

Preparation time: $1^1/_2$ hours   Cooking time: 25–35 mins
Makes approx one $1^3/_4$ lb (875g) loaf

METHOD

1. Whisk the yeast and warm water together. Leave in a warm place for 5–10 minutes to ferment.

2. Mix the flour with the salt and brewer's yeast in a bowl. Pour over the yeast mixture, shoyu and oil. Add the cooked rice.

3. Work to a smooth dough and knead well, adding more flour or liquid if necessary. Transfer to a clean bowl. Cover with clingfilm or a cloth and leave to rise for 30–40 minutes.

4. Knock back and knead briefly. Shape the dough into 1 large loaf. Place on a greased baking sheet. Cover and leave to prove for 20–25 minutes. Prick well.

5. Bake in a preheated oven at Gas Mark 7, 425°F, 220°C for 25–35 minutes. Cool on a wire rack.

Illustrated on page 44

BASIC SAVOURY BREAD

INGREDIENTS

1½oz (40g) fresh yeast
2 tsp (10ml) clear honey
1 pint (600ml) warm water
2 lb (1kg) wholemeal flour
1½ tsp (7.5ml) salt
1 tbsp (15ml) olive oil

•

NUTRITION PROFILE

This high-fibre dough is a good source of niacin, protein, Vitamins B₁ and B₆, iron, magnesium and zinc.

• Per loaf •
Carbohydrate: 223g
Protein: 45g **Fibre:** 33g
Fat: 12g **Calories:** 1125

While you are making one loaf of bread, it is a good idea to make up a large amount of basic dough, which you can then divide and make into several varieties, which could be frozen once baked.

Preparation time: 50 mins
Makes approx 3 lb (1.5kg) dough

METHOD

1. Whisk the yeast, honey and ¼ pint (150ml) of the warm water together. Leave in a warm place for 5–10 minutes to ferment.

2. Mix the flour with the salt in a bowl. Pour over the yeast mixture and add the remaining warm water and olive oil.

3. Work to a dough and knead well, adding a little more flour or water if necessary. Transfer to a clean bowl. Cover with clingfilm or a cloth and leave to rise for 30–40 minutes.

4. To make the savoury variations, add one of the fillings in the following 3 recipes to 1 lb (500g) of this basic bread dough.

ONION BREAD

INGREDIENTS

2 tsp (10ml) olive oil
1 medium onion, peeled and very finely chopped
1–2 cloves garlic, crushed
2 tsp (10ml) creamed horseradish
1 lb (500g) savoury dough (see above)

GLAZE
a little beaten egg
1 tbsp (15ml) poppy seeds

•

NUTRITION PROFILE

This loaf is a good source of protein, fibre, niacin, magnesium, Vitamins B₁ and B₆, iron and zinc.

• Per loaf •
Carbohydrate: 234g
Protein: 53g **Fibre:** 35g
Fat: 30g **Calories:** 1370

Onion bread is moist and fairly rich, so there is no need to add butter.

Preparation time: 30 mins (plus 50 mins for making the basic dough)
Cooking time: 25–30 mins
Makes approx one 1 lb (500g) loaf

METHOD

1. Heat the oil in a pan and gently fry the onion until softened but not coloured. Add the garlic and fry for 2–3 minutes. Mix in the horseradish and leave the mixture to cool.

2. Roll out the dough into a short thick oblong. Using your fingertips, make several indentations. Spoon over the onion mixture. Roll the dough around the filling and knead briefly. Shape into a loaf and place in a well-greased 1 lb (500g) loaf tin. Cover and leave to prove for 20 minutes then glaze.

3. Bake in a preheated oven at Gas Mark 7, 425°F, 220°C for 25–30 minutes. Cool on a wire rack.

Illustrated on page 47

Top: **Cashew and carrot braid** (*see p.42*); Bottom: **Rice bread** (*see p.43*).

MUSHROOM AND MUSTARD ROLL

INGREDIENTS

1 tbsp (15ml) sunflower oil
8oz (250g) mushrooms, wiped and
finely chopped
1–2 cloves garlic, crushed
1–2 tsp (5–10ml) wholegrain mustard
black pepper
½ tsp paprika
1 lb (500g) savoury dough (see p. 45)

GARNISH
a little paprika

•

NUTRITION PROFILE

*This recipe is a good source of fibre,
protein, iron, magnesium, zinc, niacin and
Vitamins B₁ and B₆.*

• Per loaf •
Carbohydrate: 232g
Protein: 54g **Fibre:** 42g
Fat: 31g **Calories:** 1370

*This spicy, high-fibre loaf makes a delicious lunchtime snack with a
salad, or a satisfying addition to a main course.*

Preparation time: 30 mins (plus 50 mins for making the basic dough)
Cooking time: 25–30 mins
Makes approx one 1 lb (500g) loaf

METHOD

1. Heat the oil in a pan and gently fry the mushrooms for 2–3
minutes so that they cook lightly but do not become too liquid.
Add the garlic and cook for 1 minute. Remove from the heat.
Drain well, then mix in the wholegrain mustard and season well.

2. Roll out the dough into a large oblong. Spread over the
mushroom mixture and roll up the dough. Place on a greased
baking sheet. Dust with extra paprika. Cover and leave to prove
for 20 minutes. Bake in a preheated oven at Gas Mark 7, 425°F,
220°C for 25–30 minutes. Cool on a wire rack.

Illustrated opposite

CHEESE AND HERB BREAD

INGREDIENTS

1 lb (500g) savoury dough (see p. 45)
2oz (50g) Cheddar cheese, grated
1 tsp (5ml) dried thyme (or 1 tsp/5ml
garlic powder)

•

NUTRITION PROFILE

*This loaf is rich in fibre, protein, calcium,
Vitamins B₁ and B₆, niacin, iron,
magnesium and zinc.*

• Per loaf •
Carbohydrate: 223g
Protein: 59g **Fibre:** 33g
Fat: 29g **Calories:** 1330

*Cheese and herbs are among the most popular accompaniments to
bread. Here, they are mixed with the dough to make a deliciously
flavoured loaf, ideal with soups and starters.*

Preparation time: 30 mins (plus 50 mins for making the basic dough)
Cooking time: 25–30 mins
Makes approx one 1 lb (500g) loaf

METHOD

1. Roll out the dough into a short thick oblong. Using your
fingertips, make several indentations.

2. Scatter over the cheese and herbs and roll up the dough, then
knead briefly.

3. Shape into a loaf and place in a well-greased 1 lb (500g) loaf
tin. Make a long slit down the dough from one end of the loaf to
the other. Cover and leave to prove for 20 minutes.

4. Bake in a preheated oven at Gas Mark 7, 425°F, 220°C for
25–30 minutes. Cool on a wire rack.

Illustrated opposite

Clockwise from top right: **Onion bread** (*see p. 45*); **Cheese and herb bread** (*see above*); **Mushroom and mustard roll** (*see above*).

SWEET YEAST BAKING

Sweet baking need not be unhealthy baking. The loaves in this section make good alternatives to cakes and biscuits at teatime. They all use unrefined flours and natural sweeteners, such as honey and concentrated apple juice, and are enriched nutritionally by the seeds, nuts and fruit.

MUESLI LOAF

INGREDIENTS
4oz (125g) dates, stoned and chopped
¼ pint (150ml) apple juice
½oz (15g) fresh yeast
2 tbsp (30ml) soya flour
3–4 fl oz (75–125ml) warm water
12oz (375g) wholemeal flour
4oz (125g) muesli (unsweetened)
½ tsp salt

GLAZE
a little beaten egg
1–2 tbsp (15–30ml) poppy seeds

•

NUTRITION PROFILE
This loaf is rich in protein, fibre, magnesium, zinc, iron, Vitamins B_1 and B_6 and niacin.

• Per loaf •
Carbohydrate: 206g
Protein: 43g **Fibre:** 29g
Fat: 19g **Calories:** 1115

This unusual loaf uses the natural sweetness of dates and apple juice for flavouring. Good for a tea bread as a healthy change from cake.

Preparation time: 1¾ hours   Cooking time: 30–35 mins
Makes approx one 1¾ lb (750g) loaf

METHOD

1. Cook the dates in the apple juice for 10–15 minutes. Beat well into a smooth purée. Leave to cool.

2. Whisk the yeast, soya flour and warm water together. Leave in a warm place for 5–10 minutes to ferment.

3. Mix the wholemeal flour with the muesli and salt in a bowl. Add the yeast mixture and cooled date purée.

4. Work to a smooth dough and knead well adding more flour or liquid if necessary. Transfer to a clean bowl. Cover with clingfilm or a cloth and leave to rise for 30–40 minutes.

5. Knock back and knead again briefly. Shape into a loaf. Put into a greased 2 lb (1kg) loaf tin.

6. Cover and leave to prove for 20–25 minutes. Brush with beaten egg and decorate with poppy seeds.

7. Bake in a preheated oven at Gas Mark 7, 425°F, 220°C for 30–35 minutes. Cool on a wire rack.

Illustrated opposite

Top: **Six-point star bread** (*see p.50*); Bottom: **Muesli loaf** (*see above*).

SIX-POINT STAR BREAD

INGREDIENTS

1/2oz (15g) fresh yeast
1/4 pint (150ml) warm milk
2 tbsp (30ml) molasses
14oz (425g) wholemeal flour
1/2 tsp salt
1 tsp (5ml) ground mixed spice
1/4 tsp ground cloves
2 eggs
2 tbsp (30ml) sunflower oil
2oz (50g) currants (optional)
2 tsp (10ml) grated orange rind
1 tsp (5ml) grated lemon rind

FILLING

3oz (75g) ground almonds
2 tsp (10ml) lemon juice
1–2 tsp (5–10ml) clear honey
1 egg yolk

GLAZE

a little beaten egg white
2 tsp (10ml) clear honey
2 tsp (10ml) concentrated apple juice

•

NUTRITION PROFILE

This recipe is a good source of Vitamins
B_1, B_2, B_6, B_{12}, *D and E, niacin,*
calcium, iron, magnesium, protein, fibre
and zinc.

• Per loaf •
Carbohydrate: 355g
Protein: 92g **Fibre:** 53g
Fat: 101g **Calories:** 2605

This is an attractive, sweet centrepiece for any festive occasion and the plaiting is not complicated once you have grasped the basic idea. The marzipan filling adds extra protein and richness. You could serve this bread plain, or with a low-sugar fruit spread.

Preparation time: 1¾ hours   Cooking time: 30–35 mins
Makes approx one 1¼ lb (625g) loaf

METHOD

1. Whisk the yeast, warm milk and molasses together. Leave in a warm place for 5–10 minutes to ferment.

2. Sift the flour with the salt and spices into a bowl. Add the yeast mixture, eggs, oil, currants and fruit rinds.

3. Work to a dough and knead well, adding more flour or liquid if necessary. Transfer to a clean greased bowl. Cover with clingfilm or a cloth, and leave to rise for 30–40 minutes.

4. For the filling, combine all the ingredients into a smooth ball.

5. Knock back the dough and knead again briefly. Divide into twelve pieces. Roll each piece into a rope and place in three groups of four ropes.

6. Plait each group of four strands until halfway up the ropes (see opposite), then fold the unplaited ends back so there are two on either side of the plait.

7. Place the three semi-plaited pieces on a greased baking sheet as if they are the spokes of a wheel (see opposite). Each plaited piece will now be separated by four loose ends. These loose ends can then be plaited together so that the whole piece has six plaited points.

8. Place the almond filling firmly in the centre of the star. Cover and leave to prove for 20–30 minutes in a warm place.

9. Brush with beaten egg white. Place a bowl of steaming water in the bottom of the oven and bake the loaf in a preheated oven at Gas Mark 7, 425°F, 220°C for 10 minutes. Reduce the oven temperature to Gas Mark 6, 400°F, 200°C and bake for a further 20–25 minutes.

10. Cool on a wire rack. While still warm, brush with a mixture of honey and concentrated apple juice.

Illustrated on page 49

MAKING SIX-POINT STAR BREAD

This decorative loaf can seem dauntingly complicated, but the only problem is plaiting with four strands instead of the more usual three. Once you get the hang of this, it is not difficult at all and the delicious flavour deserves to be complemented with an attractive appearance.

1. Take the right rope over the middle two ropes, then the left rope over the single strand into the middle.

2. Take the two right-hand ropes across into the centre. Repeat the process from the left, until half plaited.

3. Arrange the dough so that each plaited group is divided by a group of ends. Plait these into 3 more "points".

SPICED SAFFRON BRAID

INGREDIENTS

¹/₂ tsp saffron
¹/₄ pint (150ml) boiling water
¹/₂oz (15g) fresh yeast
1 tbsp (15ml) clear honey
14oz (425g) wholemeal flour
¹/₂ tsp salt
¹/₂ tsp ground cardamom
¹/₂ tsp ground cloves
1 egg
grated rind and juice of ¹/₂ orange
1–2 tbsp (15–30ml) milk (optional)

FILLING
4oz (125g) dried vine fruits
juice of ¹/₂ orange
2oz (50g) flaked almonds

GLAZE
a little beaten egg
1–2 tsp (5–10ml) clear honey
1–2 tbsp (15–30ml) flaked almonds
•

NUTRITION PROFILE

This recipe is rich in magnesium, zinc, iron, niacin, Vitamins B₁, B₆ and E.

• Per loaf •
Carbohydrate: 379g
Protein: 81g **Fibre:** 56g
Fat: 53g **Calories:** 2215

This attractive braided loaf is surprisingly easy to make. Saffron adds an appealing golden glow to the bread.

Preparation time: 1³/₄ hours   Cooking time: 25–30 mins
Makes approx one 1¹/₄ lb (625g) loaf

METHOD

1. Infuse the saffron in the water. Allow the water to cool to blood heat. Whisk in the yeast and honey. Leave in a warm place for 5–10 minutes to ferment. Mix the flour, salt and spices in a bowl. Pour over the yeast liquid and add the egg, orange rind and juice, and milk (if using). Work to a smooth dough and knead, adding extra flour or liquid if necessary. Transfer to a greased bowl. Cover and leave to rise for 30–40 minutes.

2. For the filling, soak the vine fruits in orange juice for at least 30 minutes, then mix in the flaked almonds.

3. Knock back and knead again briefly. Roll out the dough to a flat oblong. Place the filling down the centre, then mark out diagonal cuts, about 1 inch (2.5cm) wide, on either side. Weave these neatly over the filling, sealing with beaten egg.

4. Place the braid on a greased baking sheet and let it prove for 20–30 minutes. Brush with beaten egg and bake in a preheated oven at Gas Mark 7, 425°F, 220°C for 25–30 minutes. Cool on a wire rack. Top with honey and almonds while still warm.

Illustrated on page 53

SPICED SULTANA AND NUTMEG LOAF

INGREDIENTS

³⁄₄oz (20g) fresh yeast
¹⁄₄ pint (150ml) warm water
12oz (375g) wholemeal flour
4oz (125g) rye flour
¹⁄₂ tsp salt
¹⁄₂ tsp grated nutmeg
2 tsp (10ml) grated orange rind
1 tsp (5ml) grated lemon rind
4oz (125g) sultanas
4oz (125g) skimmed milk soft cheese (quark)

•

NUTRITION PROFILE

This loaf is rich in iron, zinc, magnesium, niacin, Vitamins B₁ and B₆.

• Per loaf •
Carbohydrate: 415g
Protein: 80g **Fibre:** 56g
Fat: 11g **Calories:** 1985

In this fruit bread recipe, orange and lemon complement the rye flour.

Preparation time: 1³⁄₄ hours Cooking time: 30–35 mins
Makes approx one 1³⁄₄ lb (875g) loaf

METHOD

1. Whisk the yeast and warm water together. Add 3oz (75g) of the wholemeal flour and put in a warm place for 15 minutes to ferment. Mix the remaining wholemeal flour with the rye flour, salt, nutmeg and rinds in a bowl. Add the yeast, sultanas and soft cheese. Work to a soft dough and knead well, adding more warm water if necessary. Transfer to a clean bowl. Cover with clingfilm or a cloth and leave to rise for 40–45 minutes.

2. Knead again briefly. Shape into a large cob. Make two cuts in the top. Place on a greased baking sheet. Cover and leave to prove for 20 minutes. Bake in a preheated oven at Gas Mark 7, 425°F, 220°C for 30–35 minutes. Cool on a wire rack.

Illustrated opposite

BANANA AND CAROB PLAIT

INGREDIENTS

¹⁄₂oz (15g) fresh yeast
1oz (25g) sugar
2 fl oz (50ml) warm water
12oz (375g) wholemeal flour
1 tsp (5ml) salt
3 tbsp (45ml) carob powder
2 tbsp (30ml) honey
2 bananas, mashed
1 egg, beaten
¹⁄₂ tsp vanilla essence

GLAZE
2 tbsp (30ml) sesame seeds

•

NUTRITION PROFILE

This plait loaf contains fibre, protein, Vitamins B₁, B₆ and E, niacin, iron, magnesium and zinc.

• Per loaf •
Carbohydrate: 312g
Protein: 63g **Fibre:** 43g
Fat: 25g **Calories:** 1640

For the best flavour make this moist, sweet tea bread a day ahead.

Preparation time: 1¹⁄₂ hours Cooking time: 25–35 mins
Makes approx one 1³⁄₄ lb (875g) loaf

METHOD

1. Whisk the yeast, sugar and warm water together. Leave in a warm place for 5–10 minutes to ferment. Sift the flour with the salt and carob powder into a bowl and add the honey. Pour over the yeast liquid, banana and egg (reserving a little) and vanilla essence. Work to a smooth dough and knead well. Cover with clingfilm or a cloth and leave to rise for 30–40 minutes.

3. Knead again briefly. Divide into three pieces and roll each piece to about a 12 inch (30cm) rope. Start plaiting at the centre for an even result. Place on a greased baking sheet. Cover and leave to prove for 20–25 minutes. Glaze with the reserved egg and the sesame seeds. Bake in a preheated oven at Gas Mark 7, 425°F, 220°C for 25–35 minutes. Cool on a wire rack.

Illustrated opposite

Clockwise from top left: **Banana and carob plait** (*see above*); **Spiced sultana and nutmeg loaf** (*see above*); **Spiced saffron braid** (*see p.51*).

PORTER BREAD

INGREDIENTS

¹/₂oz (15g) fresh yeast
2–3 tbsp (30–45ml) skimmed
milk, warmed
1oz (25g) muscovado sugar
12oz (375g) wholemeal flour
1 tsp (5ml) salt
2 tsp (10ml) ground mixed spices
2 tbsp (30ml) soya flour
3oz (75g) currants
3oz (75g) raisins
2 tbsp (30ml) sunflower oil
2 tbsp (30ml) malt extract
¹/₄ pint (150ml) stout ale

•

NUTRITION PROFILE

This loaf contains plenty of Vitamins B₁,
B₆ and E, niacin, folic acid, magnesium,
iron, zinc, protein and fibre.

• Per loaf •
Carbohydrate: 412g
Protein: 64g **Fibre:** 47g
Fat: 41g **Calories:** 2215

A delicious sweet, moist loaf that gains its name from stout ale. If you
prefer a soft crust, place a bowl of steaming water in the oven.

Preparation time: 1¹/₂ hours Cooking time: 25–30 mins
Makes approx one 1¹/₂ lb (750g) loaf

METHOD

1. Whisk the yeast, warm milk and sugar together. Leave for
5–10 minutes to ferment.

2. Mix the flour, salt, spice, soya flour, currants and raisins in a
bowl. Pour over the yeast mixture, oil, malt extract and stout.
Work to a smooth dough and knead well, adding a little more
flour or liquid if necessary. Transfer to a clean bowl. Cover with
clingfilm or a cloth and leave to rise for 35–40 minutes.

3. Knead again briefly. Shape the dough into a loaf. Place in a
greased 2 lb (1kg) loaf tin. Cover and leave to prove for 20–25
minutes. Brush with beaten egg. Bake in a preheated oven at Gas
Mark 7, 425°F, 220°C for 25–30 minutes. While hot, brush with
a mixture of honey and malt extract. Cool on a wire rack.

Illustrated opposite

WHEATBERRY ᴬᴺᴰ HONEY LOAF

INGREDIENTS

¹/₂oz (15g) fresh yeast
1 tbsp (15ml) clear honey
8 fl oz (250ml) warm water
12oz (375g) wholemeal flour
¹/₂ tsp salt
1 tbsp (15ml) wheatgerm
1 tbsp (15ml) olive oil
4oz (125g) cooked wheat grain

•

NUTRITION PROFILE

This bread is a good source of Vitamins
B₁, B₆ and E, niacin, protein, fibre, zinc,
iron and magnesium.

• Per loaf •
Carbohydrate: 198g
Protein: 40g **Fibre:** 29g
Fat: 17g **Calories:** 1055

A light loaf with the slightly chewy texture of cooked wheat grain. To
cook wheat grain, boil in fresh water for 1 hour.

Preparation time: 1¹/₂ hours Cooking time: loaf 25–35 mins
Makes approx one 1 lb (500g) loaf and 4 rolls

METHOD

1. Whisk the yeast, honey and warm water together. Leave for
5–10 minutes to ferment.

2. Mix the flour with the salt and wheatgerm in a bowl. Add the
yeast mixture, olive oil and cooked wheat. Knead well. Transfer
to a clean bowl. Cover and leave to rise for 35–40 minutes.

3. Knead again lightly. Shape, put the loaf in a greased 1 lb
(500g) loaf tin, and the rolls on a baking sheet, cover and leave
for 20 minutes. Bake in a preheated oven at Gas Mark 7, 425°F,
220°C, for 25–35 minutes. Cool on a wire rack.

Illustrated opposite

Clockwise from top left: **Wheatberry and honey loaf** (*see above*); **Porter bread** (*see above*); **Festive fruit ring** (*see p.56*).

FESTIVE FRUIT RING

INGREDIENTS

½oz (15g) fresh yeast
½ pint (300ml) skimmed
milk, warmed
2 tbsp (30ml) honey
1 lb (500g) wholemeal flour
3 tbsp (45ml) carob powder
½ tsp salt
1 tsp (5ml) grated lemon rind
1 tsp (5ml) grated orange rind
1 tsp (5ml) vanilla essence
2 tbsp (30ml) sunflower oil

FILLING
2oz (50g) raisins
2oz (50g) sultanas
¼ pint (150ml) orange juice
juice of ½ lemon
2oz (50g) almonds, chopped

GLAZE
2 tsp (10ml) concentrated apple juice
2 tsp (10ml) clear honey
1–2 tbsp (15–30ml)
desiccated coconut

•

NUTRITION PROFILE

*This fruit ring is a good source of protein,
zinc, magnesium, calcium, iron, fibre,
Vitamins B$_1$, B$_6$ and E and niacin.*

• Per loaf •
Carbohydrate: 482g
Protein: 91g **Fibre:** 69g
Fat: 77g **Calories:** 2880

This fruit-filled ring loaf makes an attractive centrepiece for special occasions. The carob and honey lend natural sweetness to the dough and the fruit and nut filling makes this a satisfying, nutritious and high-fibre dessert or tea bread.

Preparation time: 1½ hours   Cooking time: 30–35 mins
Makes approx one 2 lb (1kg) loaf

METHOD

1. Whisk the yeast, milk and honey together. Leave in a warm place for 5–10 minutes to ferment.

2. Sift the flour, carob and salt into a separate bowl. Mix in the lemon and orange rind.

3. Pour over the yeast mixture, add the vanilla essence and oil. Work to a dough. Knead well for 5–10 minutes. Transfer to a clean bowl. Cover with clingfilm or a cloth and leave to rise for 30 minutes.

4. For the filling, gently plump up the raisins and sultanas by warming them in the orange and lemon juice for 10 minutes in a covered pan. Add the almonds. Leave the mixture to cool.

5. Roll the dough out into a large oblong. Spread the fruit filling down the centre. Fold the dough over the top and seal with a little water.

6. Shape into a ring. Set on to a lightly greased baking sheet and cut 10–12 slashes around the outside. Leave to prove for 15–20 minutes.

7. Place a bowl of steaming water at the bottom of the oven and bake the ring in a preheated oven at Gas Mark 6, 400°F, 200°C for 30–35 minutes.

8. Brush with a mixture of honey and concentrated apple juice while the bread is still warm. Sprinkle over the coconut for decoration.

Illustrated on page 55

CONTINENTAL

All countries have their own particular bread recipes which seem to have developed intuitively over the generations. The French have croissants and brioches, the Germans pumpernickel, the Italians pizza. This section contains some healthy versions of popular traditional breads from the Continent.

PIZZA LOAF

INGREDIENTS

$^{1}/_{2}$oz (15g) fresh yeast
$^{1}/_{2}$ pint (300ml) warm water
1 lb (500g) wholemeal flour
$^{1}/_{2}$ tsp salt
1 tsp (5ml) dried oregano

FILLING
1$^{1}/_{2}$ lb (750g) onions, peeled and finely chopped
1 tbsp (15ml) olive oil
3 cloves garlic, crushed
2 bay leaves
1 tsp (5ml) dried oregano
4 tbsp (60ml) tomato purée
2oz (50g) olives, stoned and chopped
2 tbsp (30ml) capers
black pepper
2oz (50g) Cheddar cheese, grated

•

NUTRITION PROFILE

This loaf is a good source of calcium, protein, iron, zinc, magnesium, fibre, niacin and Vitamins B$_1$, B$_6$ and C.

• Per loaf •
Carbohydrate: 388 g
Protein: 94g   **Fibre:** 62g
Fat: 51g   **Calories:** 2290

This wholemeal stuffed pizza makes a nutritious snack or a tasty supper dish served with a salad. It is high in fibre and protein.

Preparation time: 1$^{1}/_{2}$ hours   Cooking time: 20–25 mins
Makes approx one 2$^{1}/_{2}$ lb (1$^{1}/_{4}$ kg) loaf

METHOD

1. Whisk the yeast and half the warm water and leave in a warm place for 5–10 minutes to ferment.

2. Mix the flour, salt and oregano in a large bowl. Pour over the yeast mixture and the remaining water. Bring to a dough then knead well for 5–10 minutes. Place in a clean bowl, cover with clingfilm or a cloth and leave to rise for 30 minutes.

3. For the filling, gently cook the onions in the oil for 7 minutes. Add the garlic, herbs, tomato purée and a little water. Cook for 20 minutes, adding more water if necessary, until the onions are well stewed. Mix in the olives and capers and season with pepper.

4. Roll out the dough into a large oblong. Cover with filling and roll up. Make four or five diagonal cuts across the surface. Cover with grated cheese. Leave to prove for 20–25 minutes.

5. Bake in a preheated oven at Gas Mark 6, 400°F, 200°C for 20–25 minutes. Cool on a wire rack and serve warm.

Illustrated on page 60

CROISSANTS

INGREDIENTS

½oz (15g) fresh yeast
1 tsp (5ml) clear honey
3 tbsp (45ml) warm water
8oz (250g) wholemeal flour
pinch sea salt
1 egg, beaten
1 tbsp (15ml) sunflower oil
2oz (50g) margarine, chilled

GLAZE
a little beaten egg

•
NUTRITION PROFILE

These croissants are a good source of iron, zinc, magnesium, Vitamins A, B₁, D and E, niacin, protein and fibre.

• Per croissant •
Carbohydrate: 21g
Protein: 5g **Fibre:** 4g
Fat: 8g **Calories:** 170

If you reduce the amount of fat in the traditional croissant version, the result is less rich but just as delicious. It is important to chill the dough well before adding the margarine so that the croissants have that distinctive flaky texture when cooked. If you want fresh croissants in the morning, leave the dough in the fridge overnight, then complete the rolling out before breakfast.

Preparation time: 2½ hours   Cooking time: 15–20 mins
Makes approx 8–10 croissants

METHOD

1. Whisk the yeast, honey and warm water together. Leave in a warm place for 5–10 minutes to ferment.

2. Mix the flour with the salt in a bowl. Pour over the yeast mixture, then add the egg, reserving a little for the glaze, and the sunflower oil.

3. Work to a soft dough and knead well, adding a little extra flour or water if necessary. Transfer to a greased bowl. Leave in the fridge for 30 minutes.

4. Roll out to a small oblong and lightly mark the dough in three. Add the margarine, by folding and rolling out (see opposite). Then turn the dough and repeat the rolling and folding, before wrapping loosely in polythene and placing in the fridge for 30 minutes.

5. Repeat using the remaining margarine, then chill again. Roll and fold once more. Roll out the dough into a large circle and divide into 8–10 wedge shapes (see opposite).

6. Roll up each wedge loosely, beginning at the widest part. Shape into a crescent. Place on a greased baking sheet. Cover and leave to prove for 15–20 minutes. Brush with the remaining egg.

7. Bake in a preheated oven at Gas Mark 7, 425°F, 220°C for 15–20 minutes. Cool on a wire rack. Serve warm.

Illustrated on page 60

MAKING CROISSANTS

The sophisticated elegance of the Continentals is epitomized by the 'petit-déjeuner français' – the French breakfast of warm croissants and freshly ground coffee. These are a healthy variation made with wholemeal flour and margarine instead of white flour and butter.

1. Roll out the dough into an oblong. Mark into 3 sections and place half the margarine on the top two-thirds.

2. Fold the bottom third up and the top third down. Quarter turn, roll out and fold again. Leave to chill, then repeat.

3. Roll the chilled dough into a large circle and divide into wedges. Roll up each one, starting at the widest part.

QUARK CROISSANTS

INGREDIENTS

½oz (15g) fresh yeast
1 tsp (5ml) clear honey
3 tbsp (45ml) warm water
8oz (250g) wholemeal flour
pinch salt
1 egg
1 tbsp (15ml) sunflower oil
4oz (125g) skimmed milk soft
cheese (quark)

•

NUTRITION PROFILE

These are a good source of protein, magnesium, iron, zinc, Vitamin B₁, niacin and fibre.

• Per croissant •
Carbohydrate: 22g
Protein: 7g **Fibre:** 4g
Fat: 3g **Calories:** 140

Here is a low-fat version of traditional croissants, based on a rich dough but filled with quark, a skimmed milk soft cheese that produces a creamy texture. These are good for breakfast or with afternoon tea.

Preparation time: 1½ hours Cooking time: 15–20 mins
Makes approx 8–10 croissants

METHOD

1. Whisk the yeast, honey and warm water together. Leave for 5–10 minutes to ferment.

2. Mix the flour with the salt in a bowl. Add the yeast mixture, egg, oil and 2oz (50g) of the quark.

3. Work to a dough and knead well, adding a little extra flour or liquid if necessary. Transfer to a greased bowl. Cover and leave to rise for 35–45 minutes.

4. Knock back and knead again briefly. Roll out the dough into a large circle and divide into 8–10 wedge shapes.

5. Spread with the remaining quark, then roll up each wedge beginning at the widest part. Shape into a crescent. Place on a greased baking sheet. Cover and leave to prove for 20 minutes.

6. Bake in a preheated oven at Gas Mark 7, 425°F, 220°C for 15–20 minutes. Cool on a wire rack. Serve warm.

Illustrated on page 60

BRIOCHE

INGREDIENTS

¹⁄₂oz (15g) fresh yeast
3 tbsp (45ml) warm water
1 tsp (5ml) clear honey
4 tbsp (60ml) skimmed milk, warmed
8oz (250g) wholemeal flour, sifted
good pinch salt
2oz (50g) margarine, melted
2 eggs
4 tbsp (60ml) soya flour

GLAZE (optional)
a little beaten egg

•

NUTRITION PROFILE

This recipe is a good source of Vitamins A, B₁, B₆, B₁₂, D and E, niacin, protein, magnesium, iron and zinc.

• Per loaf •
Carbohydrate: 184g
Protein: 73g **Fibre:** 30g
Fat: 65g **Calories:** 1570

This delicious and attractive loaf works extremely well with wholemeal flour provided that the mixture is beaten thoroughly at each stage, especially during the last 10 minutes. If it is not beaten sufficiently the loaf will be very heavy. I have cut down on the traditional quantities of eggs and fat and find that the addition of soya flour provides richness and flavour.

Preparation time: 4³⁄₄ hours   Cooking time: 30–35 mins
For one 2–2¹⁄₂ pint (1.2–1.5 litre) brioche mould

METHOD

1. Whisk the yeast, warm water and honey. Stir in the warm milk, 3oz (75g) of the flour and the salt. Beat until very well blended.

2. Stir in the melted margarine and beat again until smooth.

3. Beat in the eggs, one at a time.

4. Add the remaining flour and soya flour. Beat for at least 10 minutes.

5. Transfer to a large, greased bowl. Cover and leave in the fridge to rise for at least 4 hours, or overnight.

6. Knock back and knead again briefly. Reserve 2–3oz (50–75g) dough for the top. Put the rest of the dough into a large brioche mould.

7. Make a small indentation in the top, then mould the remaining dough into a small round and place on top. Cover and leave to prove for 20 minutes. Brush with beaten egg.

8. Bake in a preheated oven at Gas Mark 7, 425°F, 220°C for 30–35 minutes. Cool on a wire rack. Serve warm.

Illustrated opposite

Clockwise from top left: **Pizza loaf** (*see p.57*); **Croissants** (*see p.58*); **Brioche** (*see above*); **Quark croissants** (*see p.59*).

PUMPERNICKEL

INGREDIENTS

4oz (125g) kibbled or cracked wheat
$\frac{1}{2}$ pint (300ml) boiling water
$\frac{1}{2}$oz (15g) fresh yeast
3 fl oz (75ml) warm water
1 tbsp (15ml) molasses
4oz (125g) wholemeal flour
1 tsp (5ml) salt
2 tbsp (30ml) carob powder
2–3 tsp (10–15ml) celery
seeds, crushed
10oz (300g) rye flour

GLAZE
2–3 tsp (10–15ml) potato flour or
rice flour
2–3 tbsp (30–45ml) water

•

NUTRITION PROFILE

*This low-fat bread is a good source of
magnesium, zinc, iron, protein, fibre and
Vitamins B$_1$ and B$_6$.*

• Per loaf •
Carbohydrate: 207g
Protein: 30g   Fibre: 28g
Fat: 6g   Calories: 950

*Cracked wheat gives this bread the moist chewy texture of a traditional
pumpernickel, while the carob powder gives it a good colour. For extra
sourness, you could leave the dough to ferment overnight, or add a
small amount of sour dough to the basic mixture.*

Preparation time: 2$\frac{1}{2}$ hours   Cooking time: 35–40 mins
Makes approx two 1 lb (500g) loaves

METHOD

1. Put the kibbled or cracked wheat in a small bowl and pour over
the boiling water. Leave to cool until warm.

2. Whisk the yeast, warm water and molasses together. Leave for
5 minutes to ferment.

3. Add the wholemeal flour. Stir in well and leave for 30 minutes
for the yeast to become quite active.

4. Mix in the cooled cracked wheat and soaking water. Add the
salt, carob powder, celery seeds and rye flour.

5. Work to a soft dough and knead well, adding more flour or
liquid if necessary. Transfer to a clean bowl. Cover and leave in a
warm place for 1 hour to rise.

6. Knock back and knead again briefly. Divide the dough in half.
Shape each piece into a long sausage shape. Place on a greased
baking sheet. Cover and leave to prove for 20–30 minutes. Brush
with a mixture of potato or rice flour and water. Prick well.

7. Place a bowl of steaming water on the bottom shelf of the
oven. Bake the loaves in a preheated oven at Gas Mark 7, 425°F,
220°C for 35–40 minutes. Brush again with glaze after about 15
minutes cooking time. Cool on a wire rack.

Illustrated on page 64

DUTCH YOGURT LOAF

INGREDIENTS

2oz (50g) rye flakes
2 tsp (10ml) linseeds
4 fl oz (125ml) hot water
4 fl oz (125ml) warm water
1½oz (40g) fresh yeast
4 fl oz (125ml) natural yogurt
3oz (75g) wholemeal flour
12oz (375g) granary-type flour
1 tsp (5ml) salt

GLAZE
a little beaten egg
a few linseeds

•

NUTRITION PROFILE

This bread is a good source of protein, fibre, iron, magnesium, zinc, Vitamin B₁ and niacin.

• Per loaf •
Carbohydrate: 168g
Protein: 38g **Fibre:** 19g
Fat: 11g **Calories:** 885

This light, nutty-flavoured bread gains its crunchy texture from the linseeds, rye flakes and the malted wheat grain in the granary-type flour. Yogurt is a useful ingredient in breadmaking; it contributes a tangy flavour and enzymes for aiding the digestion.

Preparation time: 1½ hours   Cooking time: 30–35 mins
Makes approx two 1 lb (500g) loaves

METHOD

1. Soak the rye flakes and linseeds in 4 fl oz (125ml) of hot water. Allow to cool.

2. Whisk the yeast and warm water together and add the yogurt. Leave for 5–10 minutes to ferment.

3. Mix the flours with the salt in a bowl. Pour over the yeast mixture and add the soaked rye flakes and linseeds.

4. Work to a dough and knead well, adding a little extra flour or yogurt if necessary. Transfer to a clean bowl. Cover with clingfilm or a cloth and leave to rise for 40–45 minutes.

5. Knock back and knead again briefly. Shape the dough into two loaves. Place on a greased baking sheet. Cover and leave to prove for 20–30 minutes. Brush with beaten egg and sprinkle with linseeds.

6. Bake in a preheated oven at Gas Mark 7, 425°F, 220°C for 30–35 minutes. Cool on a wire rack.

Illustrated on page 64

ORANGE SAVARIN

INGREDIENTS

¹⁄₂oz (15g) fresh yeast
5 tbsp (75ml) warm water
1 tsp (5ml) clear honey
4oz (125g) wholemeal flour
1 tbsp (15ml) soya flour
pinch of salt
2 eggs
1oz (25g) margarine
2 tsp (10ml) grated orange rind
juice of 1–2 oranges
1–2 tbsp (15–30ml) Cointreau
or Benedictine

FILLING

3–4 oranges, peeled and segmented
1–2 tbsp (15–30ml) Cointreau
or Benedictine

TOPPING

natural yogurt or smetana
•

NUTRITION PROFILE

*This recipe provides plenty of Vitamins A,
B₁₂, C, D and E, calcium, magnesium
and iron.*

• Per loaf •
Carbohydrate: 172g
Protein: 53g **Fibre:** 22g
Fat: 37g **Calories:** 1300

*Savarin is traditionally light and airy and heavily soaked in sugar syrup,
but this healthy version is just as delicious. Wholemeal flour gives a
slightly more substantial base and the fruit juice marinade is very
refreshing. Make sure the sponge is well soaked and serve with fresh
fruit. A savarin mould is a ring mould with a rounded top.*

Preparation time: 1¹⁄₂ hours (plus 2–3 hours' soaking time)
Cooking time: 20 mins
For one 1¹⁄₂ pint (1 litre) savarin mould

METHOD

1. Whisk the yeast, water and honey together. Leave for 5–10
minutes to ferment.

2. Mix in 1oz (25g) of the wholemeal flour, and the soya flour.
Cover and leave for 30 minutes to rise.

3. Add the remaining flour, salt, eggs, margarine and orange rind.
Beat very well.

4. Pour into a lightly buttered 1¹⁄₂ pint (1 litre) savarin mould.
Cover with clingfilm or a cloth and leave to prove for 30 minutes
in a warm place.

5. Bake in a preheated oven at Gas Mark 6, 400°F, 200°C for
20 minutes.

6. Turn out and cool slightly on a wire rack. Replace in the mould
and prick the surface with a fine skewer. Pour the orange juice
and liqueur over the savarin. Leave to soak for 2–3 hours.

7. For the filling, marinate the orange segments in the liqueur and
chill.

8. Turn out the savarin and serve with the marinated oranges and
yogurt or smetana.

Illustrated opposite

Clockwise from bottom right: **Pumpernickel** (*see p.62*); **Dutch yogurt loaf** (*see p.63*); **Orange savarin** (*see above*).

FIG ᴬᴺᴰ APPLE KUCHEN

INGREDIENTS

4oz (125g) dried figs
1 lb (500g) cooking apples, peeled,
cored and chopped
½oz (15g) fresh yeast
4 fl oz (125ml) cider, warmed
10oz (300g) wholemeal flour, sifted
½ tsp salt
2 tsp (10ml) ground cinnamon
2 eggs, beaten
2 tbsp (30ml) sunflower oil
1 tsp (5ml) vanilla essence

•

NUTRITION PROFILE

*This recipe provides plenty of Vitamins
B_1, B_6, B_{12}, C, D and E, niacin, iron,
magnesium, protein, fibre and zinc.*

• Per loaf •
Carbohydrate: 321g
Protein: 60g   **Fibre:** 60g
Fat: 49g   **Calories:** 1990

*This yeast-risen cake is popular on the Continent served with morning
coffee. In this version, it is sweetened with figs which are high in
calcium and potassium. The light, airy texture comes from the eggs and
from beating the mixture thoroughly. I've cut out most of the fat used in
a traditional recipe, so if you find the kuchen a little dry, serve it with
some sugar-free jam or a low-fat spread. A kugelhopf mould is round,
with a ray-like pattern on the base and sides.*

Preparation time: 1¾ hours   Cooking time: 50–55 mins
Makes approx one 1½ lb (750g) loaf

METHOD

1. Remove the stalks from the figs and chop very finely. Stew in a
little water for 10 minutes.

2. Add the apples, cover and continue cooking for about 10
minutes until the fruit turns to a purée. Leave to cool.

3. Whisk the yeast and cider together. Leave for 5–10 minutes
to ferment.

4. Beat in half the flour and leave for 15 minutes.

5. Mix in the remaining flour, the salt, cinnamon, fruit purée,
eggs, oil and vanilla essence. Beat thoroughly until the mixture is
smooth and elastic.

6. Spoon into a well-greased 2–2½ pint (1.2–1.5 litre) kugelhopf
tin. Cover with clingfilm or a cloth and leave to rise for
45–60 minutes.

7. Bake in a preheated oven at Gas Mark 6, 400°F, 200°C for 10
minutes, then reduce the oven temperature to Gas Mark 5,
375°F, 190°C and bake for a further 40–45 minutes. If the top
becomes too crusty, lower the oven temperature or cover with
foil. Cool on a wire rack, but serve warm.

Illustrated opposite

Top: **Filled tea ring** (*see p. 68*); Bottom: **Fig and apple kuchen** (*see above*).

FILLED TEA RING

INGREDIENTS

1oz (25g) fresh yeast
1 tbsp (15ml) clear honey
¼ pint (150ml) water
1 lb (500g) wholemeal flour
½ tsp salt
2 tbsp (30ml) soya flour
1 tbsp (15ml) sunflower oil
¼ pint (150ml) apple juice, warmed

FILLING
4oz (125g) poppy seeds
4oz (125g) ground hazelnuts
2 tbsp (30ml) rum
2 tbsp (30ml) concentrated apple juice
1 tsp (5ml) lemon rind

ALTERNATIVE FILLING
1 tbsp (15ml) carob powder
8oz (250g) ground cashew nuts
1 tsp (5ml) vanilla essence
8 fl oz (250ml) apple juice
2 tbsp (30ml) sweet sherry or Madeira

GLAZE (optional)
a little beaten egg
1 tbsp (15ml) poppy seeds or finely
chopped nuts

•

NUTRITION PROFILE

*This tea ring is a good source of protein,
folic acid, fibre, iron, zinc, magnesium,
niacin and Vitamins B_1, B_6 and E.*

• Per piece •
Carbohydrate: 25g
Protein: 8·4g **Fibre:** 4·1g
Fat: 10g **Calories:** 222

With alternative filling

*This tea ring is a good source of protein,
fibre, iron, zinc, magnesium, Vitamins
B_1, B_2 and B_6, niacin and folic acid.*

• Per piece •
Carbohydrate: 29·8g
Protein: 8·3g **Fibre:** 29·8g
Fat: 9·5g **Calories:** 229

*A basic sweet dough can be filled with all kinds of ingredients and,
when rolled up, makes a most impressive tea ring. Here are two fillings
to choose from: one a traditional Jewish poppy seed and nut filling,
flavoured with rum, which has a good dark colour; the other a rather
exotic carob nut filling, flavoured with sherry or Madeira.*

Preparation time: 1¾ hours   Cooking time: 25–35 mins
Makes 16 pieces

METHOD

1. Whisk the yeast, honey and warm water together. Leave in a
warm place to ferment for 5–10 minutes.

2. Mix the flour with the salt and soya flour in a bowl. Pour over
the yeast mixture, oil and apple juice.

3. Work to a smooth dough and knead well, adding a little more
flour or liquid if necessary. Transfer to a clean bowl, cover with
clingfilm or a cloth and leave for 30 minutes to rise.

4. Meanwhile, to make either of the fillings, mix all the
ingredients thoroughly together.

5. Knock back and knead the dough again briefly. Roll out to a
large oblong. Spread over the chosen filling and loosely roll up
the dough into a sausage shape. Shape into a ring, pinching the
edges together. Make 16 cuts round the dough so that the ring
can rise evenly. Place on a greased baking sheet.

6. Cover and leave to prove for 20 minutes. Brush with beaten
egg and sprinkle with poppy seeds or nut pieces.

7. Bake in a preheated oven at Gas Mark 7, 425°F, 220°C for
25–35 minutes. Cool on a wire rack.

Illustrated on page 67

ETHNIC

The traditional breads of some countries can seem very far removed from the square loaf of one's childhood, so that the idea of making them can be rather daunting. However it really is worth the extra effort to make the bread that traditionally goes with a particular meal – poori or naan with curry, or pitta bread with kebabs.

HAMMEN TACHEN

These Jewish tricorn buns are delicious to serve at tea time. Poppy seeds provide a unique flavour and good dark colour. They can be a little bitter so I find it best to sweeten the mixture with a dried fruit purée.

Preparation time: 1½–1¾ hours   Cooking time: 15–20 mins
Makes approx 8 buns

INGREDIENTS

½oz (15g) fresh yeast
¼ pint (150ml) apple juice, warmed
1 tsp (5ml) clear honey
8oz (250g) wholemeal flour
pinch salt
1 tsp (5ml) ground mixed spice
¼ tsp ground cloves
1oz (25g) margarine, melted
1 egg, beaten

FILLING
2oz (50g) ground poppy seeds
1oz (25g) ground almonds
juice of 1 orange
3oz (75g) raisins, soaked in a little apple juice

GLAZE
clear honey

•

NUTRITION PROFILE

These buns are a good source of protein, fibre, zinc, iron, magnesium, niacin and Vitamins B₁, D and E.

• Per bun •
Carbohydrate: 31g
Protein: 7g   **Fibre:** 4g
Fat: 9g   **Calories:** 225

METHOD

1. Whisk the yeast and fruit juice together. Add the honey and leave to ferment for 5–10 minutes.

2. Mix the flour with the salt and spices in a bowl. Pour over the yeast mixture, then add the melted margarine and egg. Knead well. Transfer to a greased bowl. Cover and leave to rise for 30–40 minutes. Knock back and knead. Roll out the dough to ¼ inch (5mm) thick and cut into eight 4 inch (10cm) rounds.

3. For the filling, mix the seeds, almonds and orange juice together. Purée the raisins with the apple juice in a blender or food processor, then mix into the filling ingredients.

4. Put a spoonful of filling on each round of dough. Then fold up three sides to make a tricorn shape. Brush with honey and place on a greased baking sheet. Cover and leave to prove for 15 minutes. Bake in a preheated oven at Gas Mark 6, 400°F, 200°C for 15–20 minutes. Cool on a wire rack.

Illustrated on page 71

BAGELS

These are traditional Jewish rolls – unusual in that they are boiled before baking. Made with an egg, this recipe includes a little soya flour to enrich the dough. Wholemeal flour makes a heavier but more nutritious version than those made with white flour.

Preparation time: 1¼ hours   Cooking time: 15–20 mins
Makes 10–12 bagels

INGREDIENTS

½oz (15g) fresh yeast
1 tsp (5ml) clear honey
¼ pint (150ml) warm water
12oz (375g) wholemeal flour
1 tsp (5ml) salt
1 tbsp (15ml) soya flour
1 tbsp (15ml) soya or sunflower oil
1 egg, beaten

GLAZE
a little beaten egg
½ small onion, peeled and finely
chopped (or 1–2 tsp/5–10 ml gomashio
or sea salt)

•

NUTRITION PROFILE

*These are rich in Vitamins B₁, B₆, B₁₂,
D and E, niacin, protein, fibre, iron,
magnesium and zinc.*

• Per bagel •
Carbohydrate: 24g
Protein: 7g   **Fibre:** 4g
Fat: 4g   **Calories:** 150

METHOD

1. Whisk the yeast, honey and warm water together in a large bowl. Leave in a warm place to ferment for 5–10 minutes.

2. Add 3oz (75g) of the wholemeal flour. Stir in well and leave for 20 minutes for the yeast to activate.

3. Sift the remaining flour, salt and soya flour. Mix into the batter adding the oil and egg. Knead well. Transfer to a clean bowl. Cover with clingfilm or a cloth and leave to rise for 20 minutes.

4. Divide the dough into 10–12 pieces and roll each piece into a long thin rope, then form into a circle, pressing the ends firmly together. Cover and leave to prove for 15 minutes.

5. Bring a large pan of water to the boil. Boil the bagels, 4–6 at a time, for 5–10 minutes. They will sink at first, then rise to the top and expand. Remove from the water and drain.

6. Place on a greased baking sheet. Brush with beaten egg and sprinkle with onion, gomashio or sea salt. Bake in a preheated oven at Gas Mark 6, 400°F, 200°C for 15–20 minutes until golden brown. Serve warm or heat through, if kept until the next day.

Illustrated opposite

From top: **Hammen tachen** (*see p.*69); **Bagels** (*see above*); **Poori** (*see p.*72).

POORI

INGREDIENTS

4oz (125g) finely milled wholemeal
flour, such as pastry or chapatti flour
2oz (50g) semolina
¼ tsp salt
peanut or sunflower oil for deep frying

•

NUTRITION PROFILE

*These are a good source of magnesium,
iron, zinc, niacin and Vitamin B₁.*

• Per poori •
Carbohydrate: 14g
Protein: 2g   **Fibre:** 2g
Fat: 5g   **Calories:** 105

*Pooris, classic Indian breads, are made from a plain dough that puffs up
when cooked and are a light, crisp accompaniment to dips and curries.
Although deep-fried they need not be greasy.*

Preparation time: 1¼ hours   Cooking time: 2–5 mins
Makes approx 9 pooris

METHOD

1. Mix the flour with the semolina and salt in a bowl. Add
enough water to make a soft pliable dough. Knead well. Transfer
to a clean bowl. Cover with clingfilm or a cloth and leave for
1 hour.

2. Divide the dough into 9 pieces. Roll out each one evenly into a
small round about ¼ inch (5mm) thick (see below). Keep the
dough you are not working with under a damp cloth.

3. Heat the oil in a large pan. Test that it is hot enough by adding
a small piece of dough; it should sizzle immediately and rise.

4. Slide the poori into the oil, taking care it does not fold in half.
Keep submerged until it puffs up, then cook for 30 seconds
(see below).

5. Remove with a slotted spoon and drain on absorbent kitchen
paper. Keep warm while cooking the remaining pooris.
Serve immediately.

Illustrated on page 71

MAKING POORI

*Throughout the world people have developed breads to complement their national culinary specialities. It is
worth the extra effort of making a traditional Indian bread like poori to accompany a curry dish. Make sure
the oil is very hot before adding the poori dough or it will not cook properly.*

1. Roll out the dough into small rounds
about ¼ inch (5mm) thick, keeping
the dough you are not using covered.

2. Heat the oil until very hot.
Submerge the poori until it puffs up,
then cook for 30 seconds.

3. Remove the cooked poori with a
slotted spoon and drain on absorbent
kitchen paper.

NAAN

INGREDIENTS

8oz (250g) wholemeal flour
¼ tsp salt
½ tsp bicarbonate of soda
8 fl oz (250ml) natural yogurt

•

NUTRITION PROFILE

These breads are a good source of Vitamins B₁ and B₆, niacin, protein, fibre, zinc, iron and magnesium.

• Per naan •
Carbohydrate: 20g
Protein: 5g **Fibre:** 3g
Fat: 1g **Calories:** 105

Naan are classic Indian flat breads, made from a yogurt dough and dry-fried. Their tangy flavour goes well with spicy dishes.

Preparation time: 1¼ hours   Cooking time: 6–10 mins
Makes approx 9 naan

METHOD

1. Sift the flour, salt and soda in a bowl. Add the yogurt slowly and mix to a soft dough. Knead well and leave covered for 1 hour.

2. Divide the dough into 9 pieces. Roll each one into a round about ¼ inch (5mm) thick. Heat a thick cast-iron skillet or griddle iron until quite hot. Place each naan firmly in the pan, then keeping the heat even, fry for 3–5 minutes on either side.

3. The naan should puff up slightly and have a mottled look on the surface. For serving, keep warm wrapped in a clean cloth.

Illustrated on page 74

PRETZELS

INGREDIENTS

¼oz (7g) yeast
¼ pint (150ml) skimmed milk, warmed
8oz (250g) wholemeal flour
½ tsp salt
2oz (50g) solid vegetable fat, melted
1 tbsp (15ml) natural yogurt

GLAZE
a little milk

•

NUTRITION PROFILE

These are a good source of magnesium, protein, fibre, iron, zinc, calcium, folic acid, niacin and Vitamins B₁ and B₆.

• Per pretzel •
Carbohydrate: 11g
Protein: 2·6g **Fibre:** 1·5g
Fat: 3·4g **Calories:** 80

Originally from Alsace and Germany, pretzels are a brittle, salted, biscuit-type roll in the form of a loose knot. This healthy wholemeal version makes a good alternative to crisps and other salty nibbles.

Preparation time: 1 hour   Cooking time: 10–15 mins
Makes approx 16 pretzels

METHOD

1. Whisk the yeast and warm milk together. Leave in a warm place to ferment for 5–10 minutes.

2. Mix the flour with the salt in a bowl. Pour over the yeast mixture, melted fat and yogurt. Work to a smooth dough and knead well, adding a little more flour if necessary. Transfer to a clean bowl. Cover and leave for 10–15 minutes.

3. Knock back and knead again briefly. Divide the dough into 16 pieces. Roll out each piece into a long thin rope. Bend the loose ends over to form a 'B' shape. Place on a greased baking sheet. Cover and leave to prove for 10–15 minutes. Bake in a preheated oven at Gas Mark 7, 425°F, 220°C for 10–15 minutes. Brush with milk while still warm.

Illustrated on page 74

PITTA BREAD

INGREDIENTS

1oz (25g) fresh yeast
2 tsp (10ml) brown sugar
¾ pint (450ml) warm water
1½ lb (750g) wholemeal flour
1 tsp (5ml) salt
1 tbsp (15ml) sunflower oil

•

NUTRITION PROFILE

*These are rich in Vitamins B_1 and B_6,
niacin, protein, fibre, zinc, magnesium
and iron.*

• Per pitta •
Carbohydrate: 26g
Protein: 5g   **Fibre:** 4g
Fat: 2g   **Calories:** 135

*These pocket breads, which originated in the Middle East, can now be
bought in wholemeal varieties in the supermarket, or you can make
your own. They make excellent sandwich cases for snacks and picnics.*

Preparation time: 1¼ hours   Cooking time: 3–5 mins per batch
Makes approx 18 pitta breads

METHOD

1. Whisk the yeast, sugar and ¼ pint (150ml) of the warm water
together. Leave in a warm place to ferment for 5–10 minutes.

2. Mix the flour with the salt in a bowl. Pour over the yeast
mixture and add the remaining water and the oil.

3. Work to a smooth dough and knead well. Transfer to a clean
bowl. Cover with clingfilm or a cloth and leave to rise for 30–40
minutes.

4. Knock back and knead again briefly. Cut the dough into 3oz
(75g) pieces and shape into rolls. Roll out into oval shapes. Place
on a floured baking sheet. Cover and leave to prove for
15–20 minutes.

5. Pre-heat a heavy skillet or baking tray. Place the breads on the
hot sheet, fitting on 2 or 3 at a time.

6. Bake in the lower part of a preheated oven at Gas Mark 7,
425°F, 220°C for 3–5 minutes.

7. Wrap in a damp tea towel to cool – this gives them their
leathery look. Split and fill as required.

Illustrated opposite

Clockwise from top right: **Pretzels** (*see p.73*); **Pitta bread** (*see above*); **Naan** (*see p.73*).

QUICK BREADS,
MUFFINS
AND
ROLLS

This section comprises many all-time favourites, like Chelsea buns and muffins, as well as some less well-known ones. These sweet and savoury loaves and rolls are all nutritious and tasty.

CORN BREAD

INGREDIENTS

3oz (75g) cornmeal
3oz (75g) wholemeal flour
1½ tsp (7.5ml) baking powder
½ tsp salt
1 egg
¼ pint (150ml) skimmed milk
1 tbsp (15ml) clear honey
1 tbsp (15ml) olive oil

•

NUTRITION PROFILE

This bread is a good source of iron, magnesium, zinc and Vitamin B₁.

• Per loaf •
Carbohydrate: 125g
Protein: 28g   Fibre: 10g
Fat: 25g   Calories: 830

Cornmeal is made from maize kernels ground with some of the husks. The combination of yellow cornmeal and wholemeal flour makes a light golden bun which is quick and easy to make. You can adapt and add to this basic recipe for sweet or savoury variations.

Preparation time: 10 mins   Cooking time: 15–20 mins
Makes one 6 inch (15cm) round or nine buns

METHOD

1. Mix the cornmeal and wholemeal flour with the baking powder and the salt in a bowl.

2. Beat the egg thoroughly. Add the milk, honey and oil and beat again until well mixed.

3. Add the liquid mixture to the flour to make a soft batter. Add a little more flour if it seems too runny. Spoon into a lightly greased 6 inch (15cm) sandwich tin or 9 bun tins.

4. Bake in a preheated oven at Gas Mark 6, 400°F, 200°C for 15–20 minutes or until risen, golden brown and firm to the touch. Cool on a wire rack.

Illustrated opposite

Top: **Corn bread** (*see above*); Bottom: **Oat and buttermilk soda bread** (*see p. 78*).

OAT $\stackrel{\text{AND}}{\sim}$ BUTTERMILK
SODA BREAD

INGREDIENTS

12oz (375g) wholemeal flour
4oz (125g) porridge oats
1 tsp (5ml) salt
1 tsp (5ml) bicarbonate of soda
½ pint (300ml) buttermilk
1 tbsp (15ml) clear honey

•

NUTRITION PROFILE

This loaf contains iron, magnesium, calcium, protein, fibre, Vitamins B₁ and B₆, niacin and zinc.

• Per loaf •
Carbohydrate: 354g
Protein: 75g **Fibre:** 42g
Fat: 18g **Calories:** 1795

This unyeasted loaf is easy to make and the oats give it a lovely creamy flavour. If you want to make a smaller quantity, simply divide the ingredients in half.

Preparation time: 10 mins   Cooking time: 45–55 mins
Makes approx one 1½ lb (750g) loaf

METHOD

1. Mix the flour with the oats, salt and soda in a bowl.

2. Add the buttermilk and honey and mix quickly to a soft dough.

3. Shape into a cob and make a cross on the top. Place on a floured baking sheet.

4. Bake in a preheated oven at Gas Mark 7, 425°F, 220°C for 20 minutes, then reduce the oven temperature to Gas Mark 6, 400°F, 200°C for 25–35 minutes. Cool slightly on a wire rack and eat while still warm.

Illustrated on page 77

BARM BRACK

INGREDIENTS

1 lb (500g) currants
½ pint (300ml) apple juice
9oz (275g) wholemeal flour
1 tsp (5ml) baking powder
pinch salt
1 tsp (5ml) ground allspice
2 eggs, lightly beaten
2 tsp (10ml) grated orange rind

•

NUTRITION PROFILE

This recipe is rich in iron, copper, calcium, magnesium, zinc, niacin, Vitamins B₁, B₆, B₁₂ and D, protein and fibre.

• Per loaf •
Carbohydrate: 529g
Protein: 59g **Fibre:** 58g
Fat: 17g **Calories:** 2375

This richly fruited teabread originated in Ireland. Traditionally, the dried fruit is soaked in tea to moisten the texture, but fruit juice produces a sweeter result.

Preparation time: 15 mins (plus overnight soaking)   Cooking time: 45 mins
Makes approx one 1½ lb (750g) loaf

METHOD

1. Soak the currants in the apple juice overnight, or simmer very gently in the apple juice for 15 minutes, then leave to cool.

2. Mix the flour with the baking powder, salt and allspice in a bowl. Mix in the currants, eggs and orange rind. Stir well.

3. Put into a small, greased cake tin or a large loaf tin.

4. Bake in a preheated oven for 45 minutes at Gas Mark 5, 375°F, 190°C. Cool on a wire rack. Serve cold.

Illustrated on page 80

PRUNE ^{AND} RYE BREAD

INGREDIENTS

6–8oz (175–250g) prunes, soaked
7oz (200g) wholemeal flour
2oz (50g) rye flour
2 tsp (10ml) ground cinnamon
1 tsp (5ml) baking powder
1 tsp (5ml) bicarbonate of soda
pinch salt
2 eggs
2 tbsp (30ml) sunflower oil
2 tbsp (30ml) concentrated apple juice
$\frac{1}{4}$ tsp vanilla essence
$\frac{1}{4}$ pint (150ml) natural yogurt

•

NUTRITION PROFILE

*This high-fibre bread is also a good source
of Vitamins B_1, B_2, B_{12}, D and E,
protein, iron and magnesium.*

• Per loaf •
Carbohydrate: 272g
Protein: 56g **Fibre:** 52g
Fat: 48g **Calories:** 1690

*A delicious, dark, moist bread well flavoured with the rye flour,
cinnamon and very subtle taste of prunes. Use this recipe for a quick
tea bread. As with all soda-based breads, it is best eaten on the day
it is made.*

Preparation time: 40 mins (plus 8–12 hours soaking time)
Cooking time: 50–60 mins
Makes approx one $1\frac{1}{2}$ lb (750g) cob

METHOD

1. Stew the prunes in their soaking liquid for 20 minutes or until
tender. Drain, reserving the juice. Stone and purée in a blender
or food processor.

2. Meanwhile, mix the wholemeal flour with the rye flour,
cinnamon, baking powder, soda and salt in a bowl.

3. Beat the eggs thoroughly, then beat in the oil, concentrated
apple juice, vanilla essence and yogurt.

4. Add the liquid ingredients to the flour mixture. Mix together
thoroughly and work to a stiff dough, adding a little prune juice
if necessary.

5. Shape the dough into a cob. Place on a greased and floured
baking sheet.

6. Bake in a preheated oven at Gas Mark 7, 425°F, 220°C for
20 minutes, then reduce the oven temperature to Gas Mark 5,
375°F, 190°C and bake for a further 30–40 minutes. Serve warm.

Illustrated on page 80

POPOVERS

INGREDIENTS

5oz (150g) wholemeal flour
pinch salt
1 tbsp (15ml) sunflower oil
8 fl oz (250ml) skimmed milk
3 eggs

•

NUTRITION PROFILE

*These are a good source of protein,
calcium, iron and Vitamins B₂, B₁₂,
D and E.*

• Per popover •
Carbohydrate: 12g
Protein: 5g **Fibre:** 2g
Fat: 4g **Calories:** 100

*These light, low-fat buns should be eaten while still warm. Serve this
plain version with sweet or savoury spreads.*

Preparation time: 10 mins   Cooking time: 30–40 mins
Makes 9–12 popovers

METHOD

1. Mix the flour with the salt in a bowl.

2. Beat the oil, milk and eggs together, then pour over the flour.

3. Beat very well for at least 3 minutes. The consistency should be
like double cream; add a little more flour if necessary. Pour into
9–12 well-greased, deep bun tins.

4. Bake in a preheated oven at Gas Mark 5, 375°F, 190°C for
30–40 minutes until well risen and shrunk from the edges of
the tins. Serve warm.

Illustrated on page 83

SPICY CHEESE POPOVERS

INGREDIENTS

5oz (150g) wholemeal flour
pinch salt
1 tbsp (15ml) sunflower oil
8 fl oz (250ml) skimmed milk
3 eggs
4oz (125g) natural cottage cheese
pinch chilli powder
black pepper

•

NUTRITION PROFILE

*These are a good source of protein,
calcium, iron and Vitamins B₂, B₁₂,
D and E.*

• Per popover •
Carbohydrate: 12.2g
Protein: 6.9g **Fibre:** 2g
Fat: 4.6g **Calories:** 115

A spicy version of plain popovers.

Preparation time: 10 mins   Cooking time: 30–40 mins
Makes 9–12 popovers

METHOD

1. Mix the flour with the salt in a bowl.

2. Beat the remaining ingredients together, then pour over
the flour.

3. Beat very well for at least 3 minutes. The consistency should be
like double cream; add a little more flour if necessary. Pour into
9–12 well-greased deep bun tins.

4. Bake in a preheated oven at Gas Mark 5, 375°F, 190°C for
30–40 minutes until well risen and shrunk from the edges of the
tins. Serve warm.

Illustrated on page 83

Clockwise from top: **Barm brack** (*see p.78*); **Chelsea buns** (*see p.85*); **Prune and rye bread** (*see p.79*).

GINGER BRAN MUFFINS

INGREDIENTS

6oz (175g) wholemeal flour
2 tsp (10ml) baking powder
½ tsp salt
1 tsp (5ml) ginger
1 tsp (5ml) mixed spice
1oz (25g) bran
1 egg
2 tbsp (30ml) sunflower oil
2 tbsp (30ml) clear honey
¼ pint (150ml) skimmed milk

•

NUTRITION PROFILE

A good source of niacin, Vitamins B₁ and E, calcium, magnesium, iron, zinc and fibre.

• Per muffin •
Carbohydrate: 18g
Protein: 4g **Fibre:** 3g
Fat: 5g **Calories:** 135

Quickly prepared, sweet muffins are ideal for breakfast or tea, making a healthy, low-fat alternative to cake. They are best eaten warm on the day they are made, but will keep for a couple of days.

Preparation time: 15 mins   Cooking time: 20–25 mins
Makes approx 9 muffins

METHOD

1. Sift the flour with the baking powder, salt, ginger and mixed spice in a bowl. Stir in the bran.

2. Beat the egg thoroughly, then beat in the oil, honey and milk. Pour the mixture over the dry ingredients. Mix thoroughly.

3. Spoon the mixture into 9 well-greased, deep muffin tins.

4. Bake in a preheated oven at Gas Mark 6, 400°F, 200°C for 20–25 minutes. Eat while still warm.

Illustrated opposite

CHEESE AND PARSNIP MUFFINS

INGREDIENTS

12oz (375g) parsnips
1 tbsp (15ml) olive oil
1 medium onion, peeled and
finely chopped
2oz (50g) cornmeal
2oz (50g) wholemeal flour
1½ tsp (7.5ml) baking powder
½ tsp salt
1 egg
2 tbsp (30ml) skimmed milk
1–2oz (25–50g) Cheddar
cheese, grated

•

NUTRITION PROFILE

These muffins are a good source of Vitamins B₁, B₆, B₁₂ and C, calcium, iron, folic acid, protein and fibre.

• Per muffin •
Carbohydrate: 20g
Protein: 5g **Fibre:** 3g
Fat: 4g **Calories:** 135

Savoury muffins can be made with all sorts of vegetable purées – carrot, swede, marrow or courgette. These mixtures combine well with cheese and herbs or mild spices such as paprika. Serve these muffins with soups or salads to make a quick nutritious meal.

Preparation time: 30 mins   Cooking time: 20–25 mins
Makes approx 9 muffins

METHOD

1. Scrub or peel the parsnips and dice finely. Steam or boil for about 15–20 minutes until soft. Mash well. Meanwhile, heat the oil in a pan and gently fry the onion until soft.

2. Mix the cornmeal with the flour, baking powder and salt. In a separate bowl, beat the egg thoroughly, then whisk in the milk.

3. Mix the liquid with the dry ingredients, adding the parsnip purée, fried onion and Cheddar cheese. Mix well, then spoon the mixture into 9 well-greased, deep muffin tins.

4. Bake in a preheated oven at Gas Mark 6, 400°F, 200°C for 20–25 minutes. Serve warm.

Illustrated opposite

Clockwise from bottom right: **Cheese and parsnip muffins** (*see above*); **Spicy cheese popovers** (*see p.81*);
Ginger bran muffins (*see above*); **Popovers** (*see p.81*).

MIXED SEED MUFFINS

INGREDIENTS

3oz (75g) granary-type flour
3oz (75g) wholemeal flour
1½ tsp (7.5ml) baking powder
½ tsp salt
1oz (25g) sunflower seeds
1oz (25g) sesame seeds
1oz (25g) linseeds
1 egg
1 tbsp (15ml) sunflower oil
¼ pint (150ml) milk and water
1 tbsp (15ml) malt extract

•

NUTRITION PROFILE

*A good source of Vitamins B_1 and E,
niacin, iron, zinc and magnesium.*

• Per muffin •
Carbohydrate: 13g
Protein: 5g   **Fibre:** 2g
Fat: 7g   **Calories:** 130

Quick to prepare, these muffins can be served with sweet or savoury toppings. The seeds and malted wheat in the granary-type flour not only provide excellent texture, but valuable vitamins and minerals.

Preparation time: 10 mins   Cooking time: 20–25 mins
Makes approx 9 muffins

METHOD

1. Mix the flours with the baking powder, salt and seeds. Beat the egg. Whisk in the sunflower oil, milk and water mixture and malt extract.

2. Pour this liquid over the dry ingredients and stir thoroughly. The mixture should have the consistency of a thick batter; add a little more milk if it seems dry.

3. Spoon the batter into 9 well-greased, deep muffin tins and bake in a preheated oven at Gas Mark 6, 400°F, 200°C for 20–25 minutes. Cool on a wire rack. Serve warm.

Illustrated on page 86

RYE ^{AND} CARAWAY KNOTS

INGREDIENTS

1oz (25g) fresh yeast
8 fl oz (250ml) skimmed milk, warmed
1 tsp (5ml) molasses
8oz (250g) wholemeal flour
8oz (250g) rye flour
½ tsp salt
1 egg yolk and 1 beaten egg (reserve a little for glazing)
2 tbsp (30ml) sunflower oil
2 tsp (10ml) caraway seeds

•

NUTRITION PROFILE

These rolls are a good source of Vitamins B_1, B_6, B_{12} and E, and of niacin, protein, fibre, magnesium, iron and zinc.

• Per roll •
Carbohydrate: 31g
Protein: 6g   **Fibre:** 3g
Fat: 5g   **Calories:** 180

Rye flour is low in gluten, so needs to be mixed with wheat flour.

Preparation time: 1¾ hours   Cooking time: 20–25 mins
Makes approx 12 rolls

METHOD

1. Whisk the yeast, milk and molasses in a large bowl. Leave in a warm place for 5 minutes to ferment. Add half the wholemeal flour and stir in well. Cover and leave to rise for 40 minutes.

2. Add the remaining flour, rye flour, salt, eggs, oil and caraway seeds (reserve a few for the topping). Knead well. If the mixture is a little sticky add more wholemeal flour.

3. Divide into twelve 3oz (75g) portions. Roll out in long strips and tie each into a loose knot. Set on a greased baking sheet. Leave to prove for 15 minutes. Brush with a little beaten egg and decorate with the remaining caraway seeds.

4. Bake in a preheated oven at Gas Mark 7, 425°F, 220°C for 20–25 minutes. Cool on a wire rack.

Illustrated on page 89

CHELSEA BUNS

INGREDIENTS

2oz (50g) currants
1/4 pint (150ml) apple juice
1 tsp (5ml) grated orange rind
1/2oz (15g) fresh yeast
2 1/2 fl oz (65ml) warm milk
1oz (25g) margarine
1 egg
1 tbsp (15ml) clear honey
10oz (300g) wholemeal flour
pinch salt
2 tbsp (30ml) soya flour

GLAZE
a little beaten egg (optional)

•

NUTRITION PROFILE

*These buns are a good source of fibre,
protein, iron, zinc, magnesium,
Vitamin B$_1$ and niacin.*

• Per bun •
Carbohydrate: 22g
Protein: 6g **Fibre:** 3g
Fat: 4g **Calories:** 145

*A slightly plainer version of the classic recipe but just as popular. I find
that soaking the dried fruit makes it sweeter, helps to keep the buns
moist and removes the need for sugar.*

Preparation time: 1 1/2 hours Cooking time: 15–20 mins
Makes 10–12 buns

METHOD

1. Stew the currants in the apple juice with the orange rind for
20 minutes, then leave to cool.

2. Whisk the yeast and warm milk together. Leave to ferment for
5 minutes.

3. Melt half the margarine. Add to the yeast mixture with the egg
and honey. Beat well, adding 3oz (75g) of the flour. Leave in a
warm place for 15 minutes for the batter to ferment.

4. Beat in the remaining flour, the salt and soya flour. Draw to a
dough. Knead. Transfer to a greased bowl. Cover and leave for 30
minutes. Roll out to a large rectangle. Spread over the remaining
margarine. Drain the currants and sprinkle over.

5. Roll up the dough from the long side and cut into 1 1/2 inch
(4cm) sections. Place on a greased baking sheet (see below).
Cover and leave to prove for 20 minutes. Brush well with
beaten egg. Bake in a preheated oven at Gas Mark 6, 400°F,
200°C for 15–20 minutes.

Illustrated on page 80

MAKING CHELSEA BUNS

*Chelsea buns originate from Chelsea, London, where they were first made in the 18th century. The
traditional recipe was made from a rich dough of butter, eggs, sugar, milk and flour, but this healthier version
uses margarine, only 1 egg, natural sweeteners, skimmed milk and wholemeal flour.*

1. Roll out the dough to a large
rectangle. Spread with half the
margarine and sprinkle with currants.

2. Roll up the dough from the long side
to form a sausage shape.

3. Cut the "sausage" into 1 1/2 inch
(4cm) buns. Place sideways on a baking
sheet, leave to prove, glaze, then bake.

HOT CROSS BUNS

INGREDIENTS

½oz (15g) fresh yeast
¼ pint (150ml) milk, warmed
1 tbsp (15ml) clear honey
2 tbsp (30ml) sunflower oil
1 egg
8oz (250g) wholemeal flour
pinch salt
1 tsp (5ml) mixed ground spice
1 tsp (5ml) ground cinnamon
½ tsp ground allspice
2oz (50g) currants
1 tsp (5ml) grated lemon rind

FOR THE CROSS
2oz (50g) ground almonds
1 egg yolk
1 tsp (5ml) lemon juice
1–2 tsp (5–10 ml) clear honey

GLAZE
a little beaten egg
1 tsp (5ml) concentrated apple juice
1 tsp (5ml) clear honey

•
NUTRITION PROFILE

*These buns are a good source of fibre,
Vitamins B₁, B₂, B₆, B₁₂, D and E,
magnesium, zinc, iron, calcium and
niacin.*

• Per bun •
Carbohydrate: 39.7g
Protein: 10.8g **Fibre:** 5.7g
Fat: 14.3g **Calories:** 330

*Hot cross buns with a good spicy taste are delicious, so this recipe has
been adapted to use more spices. The almond paste for the crosses needs
to be quite well sweetened or it becomes dry once cooked – otherwise
leave the buns plain.*

Preparation time: 1½ hours   Cooking time: 15–20 mins
Makes 6–8 buns

METHOD

1. Whisk the yeast, milk and honey together. Leave in a warm
place for 5–10 minutes to ferment. Mix in the oil and egg and
beat well.

2. Sift the flour with the salt and spices into a bowl. Pour over the
yeast mixture. Work to a dough and knead well. Transfer to a
greased bowl. Cover with clingfilm or a cloth and leave to rise
for 30 minutes.

3. Knock back and knead again briefly, then work in the currants
and lemon rind.

4. Divide the dough into 6–8 pieces and shape into buns. Mark
each one with a deep cross, using a knife. Place on a greased
baking sheet. Cover with clingfilm or a cloth and leave to prove
for 20 minutes.

5. For the almond crosses, mix all the ingredients together to
form a stiff but pliable paste. Press out and cut into strips. Form
two strips into a cross shape, pressing them firmly together
where they cross.

6. Place a cross on top of each bun. Brush all over with
beaten egg.

7. Bake in a preheated oven at Gas Mark 7, 425°F, 220°C for
15–20 minutes. Brush with a mixture of concentrated apple juice
and honey while still warm.

Illustrated opposite

Top: **Hot cross buns** (*see above*); Bottom: **Mixed seed muffins** (*see p.84*).

BREAD STICKS (GRISSINI)

INGREDIENTS

¹/₂oz (15g) fresh yeast
¹/₄ pint (150ml) warm water
12oz (375g) wholemeal flour
¹/₂ tsp salt
2 tbsp (30ml) olive oil

GLAZE

a little beaten egg white
gomashio or sesame seeds

•

NUTRITION PROFILE

*These bread sticks are a good source of
iron, magnesium, zinc, Vitamin B₁
and niacin.*

• Per stick •
Carbohydrate: 16g
Protein: 4g **Fibre:** 2g
Fat: 3g **Calories:** 100

*Wholemeal Italian bread sticks are an excellent accompaniment to
soups, or for buffet-style meals. They also make a healthy alternative to
cocktail biscuits or salted nuts.*

Preparation time: 1¹/₄ hours   Cooking time: 15 mins
Makes 15–20 bread sticks

METHOD

1. Whisk the yeast and warm water together. Leave in a warm
place for 5–10 minutes to ferment.

2. Sift the flour with the salt into a bowl. Pour over the yeast
mixture and oil.

3. Work to a smooth dough and knead well, adding a little more
liquid if necessary. Transfer to a clean bowl. Lightly oil the
surface of the dough. Cover with clingfilm or a cloth and leave to
rise for 20 minutes.

4. Knock back and knead again briefly. Divide the dough into
15–20 pieces. Roll each one out into a very long rope. Place on a
greased baking sheet.

5. Cover and leave to prove for 10 minutes. Brush with beaten
egg white, then sprinkle with gomashio or sesame seeds.

6. Bake in a preheated oven at Gas Mark 7, 425°F, 220°C for
15 minutes or until quite crisp. Cool on a wire rack.

Illustrated opposite

Top: **Bread sticks (grissini)** (*see above*); Bottom: **Rye and caraway knots** (*see p.84*).